The Ozarks

The People, The Mountains, The Magic

Text and Photography
by George Oxford Miller

Voyageur Press

Other books by George Oxford Miller
The Texas Hill Country
Texas Parks and Campgrounds, third edition
A Field Guide to Wildflowers, Trees, and Shrubs of Texas
Landscaping with Native Plants of Texas and the Southwest
Texas Photo Safaris
A Field Guide to Wildlife of Texas and the Southwest

Edited by Todd R. Berger
Designed by Leslie Ross
Printed in Hong Kong

96   97   98   99   00   5   4   3   2   1

Library of Congress Cataloging-in-Publication Data
Miller, George Oxford, 1943–
    The Ozarks : the people, the mountains, the magic / text and
photography by George Oxford Miller.
        p.   cm.
    Includes index.
    ISBN 0-89658-281-7
    1. Ozark Mountains—Social life and customs.   2. Ozark Mountains
Region—Social life and customs. 3. Ozark Mountains—Description and
travel.   4. Ozark Mountains Region—Description and travel.
    I. Title.
F417.O9M55   1996
976.7'1—dc20   95–36141
            CIP

Distributed in Canada by Raincoast Books, 8680 Cambie Street, Vancouver, B.C. V6P 6M9

Published by VOYAGEUR PRESS, INC.
123 North Second Street, P.O. Box 338, Stillwater, MN 55082 U.S.A.
612-430-2210, fax 612-430-2211

Please write or call, or stop by, for our free catalog of natural history publications. Our toll-free number
to place an order or to obtain a free catalog is 800-888-WOLF (800-888-9653).

Educators, fundraisers, premium and gift buyers, publicists, and marketing managers: Looking for creative
products and new sales ideas? Voyageur Press books are available at special discounts when purchased in quantities,
and special editions can be created to your specifications. For details, contact the marketing department.

Permissions
Deane, Ernie. "Ozarks Country." *The Ozarks Mountaineer.* 1975. Reprinted by permission of Frances Deane Alexander.
Rossiter, Phyllis. *A Living History of the Ozarks.* Gretna, LA: Pelican Publishing Co., 1992. Reprinted by permission of the publisher.
Video Post Production Company. *Lights, Camera, Branson* (video). Branson, MO; Ozark Marketing Council, 1995. Quotations
printed by permission from Bobby Vinton, Tony Orlando, Yakov Smirnoff, Jim Stafford, and the Lennon Sisters.

Page 1: Ponca Wilderness Area, Newton County, Arkansas. The Ozark Mountains cannot be separated from the streams and rivers that nourish and carve the hills and hollows of the region. Sneed Creek feeds the Buffalo National River.

Acknowledgments

As with most ideas that make the difficult transition from concept to reality, my notion for a book on the Ozarks evolved significantly, with the help of many people, as the project progressed. The original intent was to capture a glimpse of the wonders of nature hidden in the remote hills and hollows of this overlooked, half-wild wilderness. But gradually, the focus of my investigation shifted toward an extended photo-essay on how the beautiful and rugged mountains have molded the people and culture of its deep valleys and meandering ridges. I realized that the more insights I received from the inhabitants, both lifetime residents and recent arrivals, the more accurately the book would reflect my intent to show, with an unsentimental view, what I observed.

Popular myth and media have stereotyped the culture and people of the Ozarks since the Depression era, when WPA photographers splashed pictures of impoverished hill folks across the nation's newspapers. As far back as 1907, people flocked to Branson to see the hillbillies described in Harold Bell Wright's bestselling novel, *The Shepherd of the Hills.* Al Capp's comic strip, "Li'l Abner," brought the daily antics of Daisy Mae and the other residents of Dogpatch into millions of homes across America, and the *Beverly Hillbillies* entertained television-watching America with the juvenile humor of the Clampetts. The roadside businesses along the narrow, ridgetop highways of the Ozarks only added to the stereotype that hillbillies were backward, ignorant relics of some bygone era. Apparently, Americans want to believe that an isolated society based on simple and pure values still exists unchanged, like the fossils in the Ozark bedrock.

Midway through this project, I began to poll Ozarkers to find out how the mountains have affected their lives. I want to thank all those who responded and helped me gain a better understanding of the deep imprint the Ozark region makes on its children. I referred to many books to gain a historical perspective of how the Ozarks have changed since the first European settlers crossed the Mississippi River and brought a new culture to the hills. I thank the authors and publishers for permitting me to use selected quotes. In documenting the explosive expansion of the music scene in Branson, I selected quotes from music celebrities from the video "Lights, Camera, Branson," produced by Video Post. I thank the celebrities for permission to use their comments from the tape in the chapter on Branson. I especially thank the members of the Ozark Society for helping me discover the natural beauty of the Ozarks.

Stone County, Arkansas. Hill folks in the Ozarks have always been known for their creative crafts, and often embellish a porch, barn, or in this case, a mailbox with their folk art.

"Say, Nature in its essence is the embodiment of my name, the Maker,
the Creator. . . . nature is God's will and is its expression in and through the contingent world."
—Bahá'u'lláh, founder of the Bahá'i Faith

Whitetailed deer, once driven almost to extinction in the Ozarks by over-hunting, now thrive in the national forests and wilderness areas.

Table of Contents

Introduction: The Quest for Authenticity

"Good logging mule, $750, 1000 lb, 10 years old."
–Sign in window of Hanking Country Store, Highway 7, Pelsor, Arkansas.

The morning rays of sun slip over the steep ridges and make a valiant effort to penetrate the mist-cloaked valleys of the Ozark Mountains. Fog hovers above the landscape like a blanket covering a sleeper reluctant to face the realities of the day. Like the people who live here, the deep hollows slowly and begrudgingly reveal the mysteries concealed behind a cloak of remoteness. But those venturing off the main thoroughfares find people who still greet visitors with a smile and treat them as neighbors. Beyond the roadside curio shops and the show-biz glitz of Branson, the Ozarks offer a rare treasure: authenticity. Just down the road from tourist attractions, such as Booger Hollow, which hypes the hillbilly image and sells made-in-Asia "Ozark" souvenirs, sits the Hanking Country Store, where you can buy a half-ton logging mule or pass the time with a fifth-generation resident who is in no hurry to get back to the chores at home.

I entered the Ozarks searching for that authenticity. I sought an unsullied landscape with streams that still run clear and people who value nature for beauty's sake. I looked for people who still possess the integrity to seal agreements with a handshake, who still value time spent sipping coffee with their friends at local cafes, and who, despite the hardships of remoteness, low income, and limited opportunities, possess a grateful appreciation for life. Most importantly, I wanted to reflect the soul of the Ozarks truthfully, without sentimentality, with a clear eye that not only sees, but also feels, responds, and reports faithfully.

In the Ozarks, I found a celebration. I found people gathered around the town square playing banjos, guitars, and dulcimers, and singing simply because their spirits yearned for expression. I found people proud of their crafts, even though the money they received could never recompense the hours and skills required to produce such works of art. And I found rivers and streams and caves and pure air and starry nights. I discovered the grandeur of mountains with distant vistas and the intimacy of tiny streams and trickling waterfalls. And I discovered an authenticity that comes only from a landscape and lifestyle that value the good inherent in nature and the inherent good in human nature.

G. O. M., June, 1995

Above: Johnson County, Arkansas. Unpaved roads lead the way to unexpected discoveries in the 1.1-million-acre Ozark National Forest and the 1.5-million-acre Mark Twain National Forest.

Opposite: Logan County, Arkansas. At an elevation of 2,753 feet, Mount Magazine, the tallest point in the Ozarks, offers hiking, camping, and spectacular views of the surrounding Ozark National Forest.

The Intimate Ozarks

"There in an empire of their own, far removed from the conventionalities the disadvantages and the problems of 'civilization,' they are living the peaceful, free and easy life that they lived 50 years ago, and that they will continue for a 100 years to come."
–Wayman Hogue, 1932, Back Yonder, An Ozark Chronicle.

"The world has grown too small for any people to live in harmless isolation."
–Dalai Lama, in exile in France.

Above: Stone County, Arkansas. Log houses and barns, many still in use, are sprinkled across the countryside along the backroads of the Ozarks.

Opposite: Logan County, Arkansas. Mist-covered Mount Magazine supports many wildflowers, such as this vetch, and rare species, such as the maple-leaf oak, which grows nowhere else in the world.

Ponca Wilderness Area, Newton County, Arkansas. Jim's Bluff on the Buffalo National River is a popular pullout for canoeists. The meandering river, once threatened by plans for a dam, is now protected by its National River designation.

"Falling water. Falling water over stone. The sound of falling water. The river rocks, smooth and round and flat, that you can't resist cradling in your palm. Six crows barking at a hawk in the sky. The differential shadows of the leaves, illusion and illumination. Peace in these old mountains, these lost and forgotten ranges."

—Jack Butler, Director of Creative Writing, College of Santa Fe, and author of *Living in Little Rock with Miss Little Rock*.

A Wilderness Reborn

Looking across the vista from the Highway 7 pullout, I can see a landscape chiseled by 300 million years of weathering at the hand of nature. In this section of the Arkansas Ozarks, forests unbroken by pastures, clear-cuts, or the shiny, tin roofs of ridgetop homesteads stretch as far as the eye can see. The tree-covered slopes of steep hollows twist along with the streams that carved them, and the hazy, green silhouettes of distant ridge lines fade into blue sky. This land has recovered valiantly from the first 150 years of Anglo settlement and exploitation.

The first pioneers swarmed to the Ozarks like ants to a picnic basket. They arrived with double-bladed axes, crosscut saws, and mule-drawn plows. They penetrated the wild mountains with two-rut "wilderness roads," then cleared narrow corridors for the advancing railroad. The railroad opened the remote mountains, with their virgin hardwood forests and hidden mineral deposits, to

exploitation by the eastern barons and to the floodtide of westward-bound settlers looking for a fertile piece of earth and the promise of prosperity. The tycoons
exploited and the settlers overpopulated, then both moved on westward toward
new, virgin territory. Creeping into their tracks, nature slowly reclaimed its own
and reforested much of the abandoned countryside.

The human hand remolds the landscape as deftly as any natural process, but
in a blink of geological time. The mortal sculpting of the Ozarks began with the
first ax blow to a virgin oak and continues today in unprotected areas, only at a
more restrained pace. Now, bulldozers scrape away ancient forest cover to provide
habitat for humanity's ruminating companion, the cow. Saws, once hand drawn
and now gasoline powered, whittle away at the second-growth forests like old
men who judge their worth by the shavings accumulated at their feet. The fertile
valleys succumbed long ago to the cutting edge of civilization. Land too steep or
poor of soil to benefit the saw, cow, or plow faces another threat: the waters of
artificial lakes. Rippled by the wake of power boats, the lakes reflect blue sky and
billowing clouds like a distorted mirror. Beneath the lifeless waters lie deep hollows that once harbored plant and animal species that had called the Ozarks home
since the last glaciers retreated north to their Arctic origins.

Newton County, Arkansas. The runoff of
spring and fall rains create many
impromptu waterfalls in the Ozarks, such
as this one plummeting to the foot of
King's Bluff.

Humans may have tamed the Ozarks with a network of paved roads, impounded the flow of its streams, and diminished the diversity of its wildlife, but
the mountains have yet to surrender their essence to the demands of a burgeoning population. The expanse of unbroken forests seen from White Rock Mountain still inspires; the rapids of the Buffalo and Current rivers still challenge; and
unnamed wilderness waterfalls and sculpted rock formations in the Mark Twain
and Ozark National Forests still thrill hikers with the sense of discovery. Centered
within a few hundred miles of the geographical heartland of the United States,
the Ozarks possess the same wilderness authenticity found in the mile-high mountains of the West, the secluded swamps of the South, and the boreal forests of the
far North.

A land rocky to its core, convoluted by sinuous ridges, and deeply dissected
by streams holds tenaciously to its identity. The prairies bordering the Ozarks to
the north, east, and west could not resist the forces of change. Plows carved the
fertile soil into fields of corn, wheat, cotton, and soybeans. But hills of stone resist
change as land with a belly soft from a thousand years of accumulated humus
cannot. The limestone and sandstone bedrock imparts its resistance to change to
the human culture that grows in the shadow of its remote hollows and serpentine
ridges. Sociologists classify the Ozarks as a "semi-arrested frontier," a land that
only slowly relinquishes its grasp on the lifestyle and values of the past.

On an Arkansas map, the highway from Marshall to Pelsor looks like a dis-
carded tangle of string. Heading west, it meanders through a picturesque valley
dissected by Bear Creek. A cable walking bridge traverses the creek, and aged
barns and buildings rest in various stages of decay like shipwrecks on an abandoned beach. The pioneers "settled up" valleys like the one cut by Bear Creek
first, clearing the forest for cropland. The adjacent valley is named Richland,
because of its rich soil, deposited over centuries of slow but certain erosion of the
surrounding hills. Today, cattle have replaced corn, but the clearing of forests

Ponca Wilderness Area, Newton County, Arkansas. The small springs and seeps that abound in the Ozarks support a lush growth of plants and flowers, even during the driest summers.

"When I think of the Ozarks, I think of water. Water's every-where—springs, creeks, waterfalls, swimming holes—and it carries the magic of the region. Put me on an Ozark gravel bar with plenty of skipping rocks, and I'm in heaven."
—Joe David Rice, Tourism Director, Arkansas Department of Parks and Tourism.

continues, creeping up the hillsides year by year like the killing waters of an impounded lake.

The blacktop winds its way through the bottomland and passes through a settlement called Canaan, Arkansas. To early settlers, weary from trudging across one rugged hollow after another, the narrow valleys must have looked like the Promised Land. Place names like Jerusalem, Mount Zion, and Mount Judea (pronounced "Mount Judy") abound. The steep, wooded slopes and rocky streams closely resemble the terrain of the Appalachians in Tennessee, North Carolina, and Kentucky. The similar topography convinced westward-bound settlers to stop and carve out a niche in the new, but hauntingly familiar, frontier.

The first non-natives in the area, French Creole trappers, settled along the Mississippi and worked the streams pouring out of the Ozarks for beaver and other fur-bearing creatures. But the trappers were too few and too transient to exert any lasting influence on the land or existing Native American cultures. Then, in 1803, the United States acquired Arkansas and Missouri through the Louisiana Purchase. Even though an 1808 treaty forced the Osage Indians to give up their legal claim to all land between the Missouri and Arkansas Rivers, the Ozarks began to fill with Native Americans displaced from the east. The first bands of Cherokees left their farming communities in the Smoky Mountains and sailed down the Tennessee River to the Mississippi and then up the Arkansas. An 1817 treaty gave them the land between the Arkansas and White Rivers, the most rugged terrain of the Ozarks. In 1819, the Kickapoo tribes deeded their land east of the Mississippi for land in the Ozarks. Delaware, Shawnee, and other eastern bands of Native Americans sought the safety of the remote mountains and shared the Ozarks with its original inhabitants: the Osage, Illinois, Caddo, and Quapaw.

Eventually, actions culminating in the Trail of Tears purged all Indians from both their ancestral homelands and acquired treaty lands and drove them farther west into Oklahoma Territory. By the mid-1830s, the Ozarks were an open frontier for settlers heading west. Pioneers reached the rich valleys with their crystal-clear streams and decided that California was too far away. They unpacked their wagons and imprinted the hills and hollows with their English and Scotch-Irish, Protestant traditions. Following the principle that the first in time is the first in importance, this culture still dominates life in the Ozarks today.

From Canaan, the highway zigzags south, then north, like a fluttering leaf. It follows Bear Creek and eventually climbs back atop a winding ridgetop. I saw the first of many mules in the two-house community of Welcome Home. The name Welcome Home fires the imagination to conjure up multiple reasons for such a name—perhaps the prodigal child returning home or a son returning from war.

The names of many towns have a curious, historical significance in the Ozarks. Snowball, near Welcome Home, was named after a community meeting hall constructed by a man named Snow. The structure became known as the Snow Hall, and in honor of this building, the town chose that name when it petitioned for a post office. Whether due to illegible writing, poor spelling, or clerical error, the name came back Snowball, and it remains unchanged today. Similarly, a community several ridges over was so remote that the townspeople decided on the

name Isolated. Phonetic spelling of hillbilly dialect resulted in the community becoming Iceledo, now a label on an unnamed dirt road shown only on topographical maps.

Upper Buffalo Wilderness Area, Newton County, Arkansas. Whitaker Creek, a tributary of the Buffalo National River, cuts a winding path through the dense forests of the Ozarks.

The blacktop highway meanders along the ridgetop, first due south, then due north through Tilly, and then twists south again at Witts Spring. On the broad, rounded ridges, you are likely to pass additional pastures with mules. The forests on the ridgetops were the first casualties of the unbridled exploitation of the virgin hardwoods after the Civil War. To the settlers flooding into the state from the mountains of the southeastern United States, the Ozarks represented a seemingly unlimited hardwood and pine-hardwood forest. Concurrently, the westward advance of railroads created an almost insatiable demand for ties, as well as an artery to transport milled lumber to eastern markets.

The felling of the forests produced great fortunes for a few timber barons, and an abundant source of cheap, cleared land for settlers. In the 1890s, timber companies could mill a thousand board feet of lumber for $2.60 and sell it for $55. The largest pine mill in the world operated at Grandin, Missouri, near Poplar Bluff. Timber was so plentiful, the mills selected only the highest quality trees and then burned the remaining forest to stimulate new growth. When the countryside was timbered out, the mills packed up and moved on, selling the charred, denuded land for $3.50 to $12.50 an acre to itinerant mill workers hankering to stay and farm.

Zinc and lead mines also thrived throughout the Ozarks. So many prospectors rushed to a new settlement along the Buffalo River when zinc was discov-

Johnson County, Arkansas. The fruits of the elderberry add a final splash of color to the forest after winter strips the leaves from the trees. Cooked, ripe elderberry is edible, but when uncooked or unripened, it is somewhat toxic.

"Nowhere else in the central United States can one find such a diversity of native plants and animals than in the Ozarks. Spring-fed meadows, rocky glades, cliffs, clear blue springs, and shaded and sheltered forests abound with native plants and animals in a nearly unequaled richness. Living here makes one acutely aware of the need to conserve these resources for our children."

—Blane Heumann, Missouri Nature Conservancy.

ered in 1880 that the boomtown was named Rush. It prospered through World War I, then gradually faded until it lost its post office in the 1950s. The largest lead deposit in North America rests in the Salem and Potosi districts of the Mark Twain National Forest in Missouri. The remaining mines in the Ozarks produce more than 80 percent of the lead currently extracted in the United States.

The cleared ridgetops and valleys were so fertile that by the early 1900s the Ozarks had become the berry bowl of the nation. Farmers raised strawberries, blueberries, and blackberries, as well as peaches and tomatoes. A seasonal lifestyle developed, with workers migrating with the crops as they ripened. But eventually the depleted, eroded soil could no longer support the berries or other crops, and farmers turned their land into pasture and seeded thousands of acres in fescue grass. They regularly burned the forests to eliminate understory shrubs and to stimulate growth of tender, young grass.

The clearing and burning of the forests, as well as relentless hunting, decimated the wildlife. In 1932, Wayman Hogue wrote in *Back Yonder, An Ozark Chronicle,* "Arkansas is known as the Bear State. Great numbers lived in the mountains of the Ozarks. The bear is omnivorous and stole many of our pigs, but he was most destructive when he got in our corn field. We hunted bear not only for the depredations he committed, but because we like bear meat. . . . Other ferocious animals denned and roamed about us, among them the wolf and wildcat . . . but they were not considered dangerous like the painter [panther]. . . . One explanation of this is that the mountains abounded plentifully with smaller game on which they could easily prey."

By the time Hogue wrote his chronicle, turkeys, panthers, wolves, and bears had all but disappeared from the Ozarks, as had beaver, elk, and bison. By the 1930s, only thirty-five hundred whitetailed deer remained in the entire state of Missouri. The town of Oil Trough, Arkansas, still carries the name inspired by a rendering plant for bear fat, though the plant disappeared at the turn of the century.

With the eradication of game animals, and the depletion of the forests and soil fertility, the once burgeoning human population of the Ozarks plummeted. Many small farmers abandoned their exhausted farms and dried-up springs and continued their march west. The federal government began buying the tax-delinquent land and established the 1.1-million-acre Ozark National Forest in 1908, and the 1.5-million-acre Mark Twain National Forest in 1945. But many with productive farms remained, and private inholdings are numerous today, especially in valleys and on ridgetops.

Lumbering, now of second-growth forest sixty to one-hundred years old, is still a vital industry in the Ozarks. Oak-hickory forests, with saw timber valued at $1.5 billion, cover 4.2 million acres of the Arkansas Ozarks. Small saw mills with stacks of 4x4 lumber or hardwood pallets dot the landscape, tucked into hollows or perched on ridges.

At Witts Spring, the two-lane highway twists 180 degrees south with the ridge line and loops around Raspberry Knob, a steep, rounded mountain, then heads north like a spring goose to the community of Ben Hur, named after the famous novel written by Lew Wallace. Ben Hur boasts four occupied homes and a Free Will Baptist Church with a his-and-her's flush outhouse. From there, the highway takes a course due west along a ridge overlooking the deep drainage of the Illinois Bayou.

An easily missed sign along the road west of Ben Hur designates a small gravel parking lot with a trail to two of the hidden wonders of the Ozarks: a one-mile loop trail leads to Kings Bluff and another to Pedestal Rock. Exposed sandstone strata form a 150-foot-high bluff, which includes the two outcroppings and winds midway along the slope of the precipitous valley. Weathering has cracked and carved the pliable sandstone into hollowed rock shelters, crevice caves, and free-standing pedestal formations.

If you are adventuresome enough to get out and explore beyond the beaten path, you can experience the thrill of discovery that still exists in the deep woods and steep hollows of these mountains. One appeal of the Ozarks is that it comprises one large discovery zone. Several natural arches and other bizarre formations lay hidden along unmarked roads in the Ozark and Mark Twain National Forests, and caves abound in the limestone bedrock of the Salem and Springfield Plateaus. Unlike a national park where you know that millions of visitors have trudged the same path and taken the same photos as you, the wonders of the Ozarks remain relatively unknown, often even to those living in nearby towns.

Several people over the last twenty years have used the same word to describe their fascination with the Ozarks: *intimacy*. The Rockies may have vastness and grandeur, but the Ozarks possess the intimacy of accessibility. You can look across a ridge to a distant valley, and know that you can hike there in hours, not the days required to traverse the expansive vistas of the West. Yet despite the intimacy, the mystery remains. The allure of anticipated pleasures tempts the visitor to explore the cascading streams and hidden valleys in search of the delights of once-blemished, but now recovered, nature.

In the fall, the seed heads of dried grass catch the sun and decorate the roadsides in the Ozarks like tiny pom-poms.

A Half-Wild Wilderness in the Heartland

"I live in the Ozark Mountains, born and raised here. . . . I have everything in the way of conveniences on my farm in Newton County [Arkansas] that they have in Chicago. I have a television and git good reception. I have a dial-system telephone. I can call anywhere in the world and talk on it. I have electricity. We can open the refrigerator and have ice cream. And at the same time, we can just turn around and in 10 minutes be back in the primitive, jist like it was when the Indians lived here."

—J. Veatle Waters at his home in Hasty, Arkansas, as told to Dr. Roy Thomas.

Above: Ponca Wilderness Area, Newton County, Arkansas. The wet-season waterfall at Hemmed-In Hollow plummets approximately 190 feet down the limestone cliff, making it the tallest waterfall between the Rockies and the Smokies.

Opposite: Ponca Wilderness Area, Newton County, Arkansas. Big Bluff towers five hundred feet above the Buffalo National River. The mixture of challenging rapids and tranquil paddling beneath such scenic bluffs attracts canoeists from around the nation.

Newton County, Arkansas. Granny Eva Henderson's cabin stands as a silent testament to a life of hardship farming the rocky soil along the Buffalo National River. Her milled-lumber house still stands in the Ponca Wilderness Area.

Granny Henderson's Cabin

Granny Eva Barnes Henderson has not sat on her front porch in two decades, but you can still enjoy the view that nourished her for seventy years. When Congress created the Buffalo National River, the eighty-three-year-old woman lived alone, except for her dog Bobby, in a clearing above Jim's Bluff, a popular pullout for canoeists. It is easy to imagine her rocking back and forth after a long day and watching the setting sun paint the landscape with the warm tints of evening light. The panorama encompasses an outcropping of rocky bluffs about halfway up the opposite ridge, as well as the grand semicircle of the Buffalo River valley. The ridge curves from left to right in a 180-degree sweep, with slopes covered by unbroken forest. It rises about thirteen hundred feet above the river and Granny's picturesque home.

Today, the gentle greens of spring brush the landscape with subtle hues and tones. Billowing clouds roll over the ridge and threaten showers later in the evening. Shadows and sunlight dapple the mountains, and the river whispers in the distance. Crows calling overhead and turkey vultures circling on the fading thermals complete the scene. Life doesn't get much more peaceful than this. Unless, of course, you have to take care of a yard full of chickens, cows, and hogs, as well as tend the garden, orchard, and house, hauling water a quarter mile up a steep hill.

Granny Henderson was no stranger to hard work. A sign on the house, which includes her picture, quotes her as saying she spent her days doing "chores, chores,

chores, and more chores." Her photograph shows a worn, wrinkled, but contented expression as she stands beside a blooming rose bush in her yard. She apparently drew sustenance from beauty, both natural and cultivated.

Granny Henderson had accumulated a lifetime of personal history in these woods by the time the Buffalo National River was established in 1972. Granny is further quoted on the sign out front: "I remember helpin' clear these fields and hammerin' up many o' these buildings. Things you work so hard doin', seems t' me, ought to be allowed to last forever." Life was simpler in Granny's youth. All a family needed was a spring for water, a source of wood for fuel and building material, and about five acres of tillable land per person for crops. In addition, a few domestic animals for table meat and for easing the work load made life a little less uncertain. Peach and apple trees still grow in Granny's front yard. Her house, elegantly constructed with milled lumber, is still watertight and sound, but the barn has collapsed. Nature slowly reclaims her own. Despite Granny's feelings, nothing of human origin in these woods lasts forever.

Pioneers settled the wilderness and carved out their niches, but after several generations of struggling with marginal and increasingly infertile farmland, many gave up and moved on. However, some pioneers continued to mine for lead and zinc, some timbered the forests, and some, like Granny Henderson, scratched out a living wherever they found pockets of fertile soil.

You will pass a half dozen or so old homesteads on the 6.5-mile trail between the Center Point and Compton trailheads leading through the Buffalo River valley to Hemmed-in Hollow. A chimney, a concrete spring house, a rusted car chassis, a one-room log cabin, and patches of irises alone in the woods are all reminders of the times when children's laughter echoed through the woods and smoke from cookstoves crowned the hollows as evening progressed.

I first heard of Hemmed-in Hollow before I ever hiked a trail or floated a stream in the Ozarks. The hollow's claim to fame is a waterfall that plummets to the base of a horseshoe-shaped box canyon. The 177-foot (some say 190-foot) sheer drop makes it the tallest waterfall, when flowing, between the Appalachians and the Rockies. I located it on wilderness maps and twice tried unsuccessfully to canoe to the mouth of the canyon (first the river flooded, then it dried up).

If you give up on floating, as I did, you can day hike or backpack into the heart of the Ponca Wilderness on the upper Buffalo River and find this elusive natural wonder. After fording several creeks and trudging up steep, muddy trails, you look up from your labored steps and there it is, a ribbon of lacy water pouring through a deep notch in the cliff. The wind whips the stream back and forth across the rusty calcite-stained cliff and wafts the spray down the narrow canyon. The play of the waterfall in the wind is mesmerizing, like watching an errant pendulum count time with random swings.

After spending the day exploring the hollows with crystalline creeks plunging from ridgetop to river bottom, I camp near Granny Henderson's house. At nightfall, the anticipated thunderstorm rolls over the ridge and chases me onto her wide front porch. I discover that I am not alone. The empty house is at full occupancy. Mice scamper through the walls, bats fly from the attic window, and

Reynolds County, Missouri. Old trucks, tractors, and cars dating back to the Great Depression still sit in abandoned fields and dilapidated sheds across the Ozarks.

"My roots run deep in the Ozark Mountains. Growing up in the Ozarks means you never escape the spell cast by the pristine streams, rugged bluffs, deep, remote hollows, and the sights and sounds of wild things. Every return is a homecoming."
—Steve N. Wilson, Director, Arkansas Game and Fish Commission.

19

Newton County, Arkansas. Swimming holes bring a cool respite to the hot summers in the Ozark Mountains. Canoeists sometimes cannot resist trying to shoot the Falling Waters waterfall in the Ozark National Forest.

"These mountains can hide you from whatever you need to forget. These valleys can show all you need to remember. These roads can take you wherever you need to go. And these creeks can serenade your journey."
—Donald Harington, author of nine novels.

a skunk forages beneath the floor. As coral berry bushes and briars creep upward and assorted critters move in, nature slowly advances the cycle from wilderness to farm and back to wilderness again.

A Wilderness Island

Wilderness came first to the Ozarks by the grace of God. Now it depends on the goodwill of humanity. After the Ozark Society won the fight to save the Buffalo River from the Army Corps of Engineers and real estate speculators, which I will describe later, conservationists lobbied Congress to establish additional wilderness areas to preserve the watershed from development. Today, seven official wilderness areas exist within the Ozark National Forest and seven more within the Mark Twain National Forest. With the protection afforded by the Wild and Scenic River Act, the Ozark National Scenic Riverways, and numerous recreation areas, state parks, and natural preserves, a portion of the wilderness that once covered the fifty-five-thousand-square-mile Ozark Plateau has returned to stay.

This half-wild wilderness lies in the heart of America like a jewel in a box of sand. The Ozark Mountains, along with the Ouachitas in central Arkansas, form a midcontinental island surrounded by prairie and pastures to the north and west, and delta farms to the south and east. The Missouri, Mississippi, and Black Rivers form its northern and eastern boundaries, and the Grand and Arkansas Rivers roughly mark its western and southern limits.

The Ozarks were born from the fire of volcanism, eroded by torrents of rain from the moist glacial climate, jolted by the shock of earthquakes, and sculpted by springwater pouring from its fractured, limestone heart. Once the Earth had but one vast land mass, Pangaea, with an unbroken forest spanning the ancient continent. Three billion years ago the Saint Francois Mountains rose to lofty heights in Missouri, but eventually were eroded down to knobs. By 600 million years ago, a series of seas inundated the Ozark region, and over time, deposited thousands of feet of limestone, shales, and sandstone sediments. Then, 280 million years ago, during the formation of the Appalachians, a massive batholith of billion-year-old granite domed up beneath Saint Francois County, Missouri, elevating the Ozark Plateau four thousand feet above the inland sea. Once again, time wore down the plateau to a featureless plain.

Remnants of that ancient granite plug are exposed in Iron County, Missouri. Elephant Rocks State Park, a small exfoliation dome and popular site for picnics and family outings, preserves the unusual formations created by the weathered granite boulders. Just across the county line at Johnson's Shut-Ins State Park, the Middle Fork of the Black River cuts a scenic gorge with waterfalls, potholes, and rapids through a strata of igneous rhyolite.

Pangaea split around 165 million years ago. North America then drifted away like a lost sailor, taking its share of biological treasures. As the climate changed through the eras, the forests, prairies, deserts, and swamps of the new continent evolved distinct differences from their increasingly distant ancestors.

Iron County, Missouri. Weathering has sculpted the billion-year-old pink granite of the Ozark Dome, an underground upwelling that once elevated the Ozarks thousands of feet, into bizarre shapes at Elephant Rocks State Park.

Sixty-three million years ago, colliding tectonic plates formed the Ouachita Mountains and elevated the Boston Mountains an additional five hundred feet. Several more uplifts followed. With each rise in elevation, the rivers, which had formed meandering channels on the flat Ozark plains, cut further into their established riverbeds. They etched deep, serpentine valleys instead of the long, straight gorges normally associated with river flow accelerated by uplifting, such as the Grand Canyon. By the Quaternary Period, one million years ago, formation of the primary subdivisions of the Ozarks—the Salem and Springfield Plateaus and the Boston and Saint Francois Mountains—and the twisting, meandering rivers were complete. The torturously dissected ridges and valleys of the Ozarks result from the slow, cutting knife of erosion, not the cataclysmic eruptions and tectonic uplifts that formed the Appalachians, Rockies, and Cascades. Stand on a knob, backbone, or ridgetop in the Ozarks and you see the level horizon of a vast plateau; look at the exposed rocks in a road-cut and you see parallel strata stacked like cake layers, not the contorted, twisted mass in the nearby Ouachitas, which has more violent origins.

The Ozark Plateau has withstood radical changes since its formation. Seas surged up the Mississippi Rift to the base of the plateau, but never inundated it. Glaciers crept as far south as the Missouri River, but their frozen fingers never gripped the hills and hollows. A moist forest covered the Ozark Mountains eleven thousand years ago as glaciers pushed boreal plants southward with the advancing colder climate. Mastodons, saber-toothed cats, giant ground sloths, and six-foot beavers roamed the dense woodlands and left their bones to fossilize in caves and crevasses.

As the glaciers retreated seven thousand years ago, cool, dry deserts replaced boreal forests, and mice replaced mammoths. Cacti, yucca, and other drought-tolerant plants from the west colonized the dry ridgetops and exposed slopes. The eastern forests retreated to the Appalachians. Like the landforms, the climate changed radically. But this time, not all the plants and animals changed.

Today, the deep hollows, steep escarpments, and dissected valleys of the Ozarks preserve a series of biological time slices like pages of a family album stretching back to the Pleistocene Epoch, one million years ago. Relic populations of plants and animals representing past climatic periods find microniches in the protected valleys that suit their requirements for survival. Isolated in the heartland, beech, witch hazel, sugar maple, and other forest species typical of the Appalachians merge with members of the dry western woodlands. Prairie wildflowers grow alongside cacti, and flooded sinkholes harbor tupelo, cypress, and other swamp plants in the midst of mountain uplands. The Ozarks also support species found nowhere else in the world. These unique plants and animals live in isolation, hundreds of miles from their closest relatives.

Of the 160 species of fish in the Ozarks, thirteen are endemic. Many of the spring and cave systems riddling the limestone mountains support their own unique populations of blind fish, salamanders, snails, crickets, and other invertebrates, as well as the endangered Ozark big-eared bat. About five hundred big-eared bats inhabit one nursery cave and one hibernation cave in Arkansas. Two other endangered cave inhabitants, the Indiana bat and the gray bat, survive in only a handful

Above: Franklin County, Arkansas. Fern and moss create a living carpet on the moist slopes of White Rock Mountain in the Ozark National Forest.

Opposite: Barry County, Missouri. Twenty million gallons of water a day flow over a cliff to form the headwaters of Roaring River and the trout hatchery in Roaring River State Park.

"The quite and calm of a cool, moist Ozarks cliff dripping with ferns and lichens and mosses is a splendid thing to behold. It is both a place to relax, knowing that a healthy environment can be maintained in a busy world of industry and agriculture, and a reminder of the diverse collection of native plants and animals to which we have inherited stewardship responsibilities."
—Blane Heumann, Missouri Nature Conservancy.

"The Ozark Mountains maintain my perspective. Returning home from my travels, I am engulfed with the beauty of the mountains, bluffs, vistas, rivers, and streams. I breathe a deep sigh and say to myself, 'Yes, this is how it was intended.'"
—Phyllis K. Speer, Arkansas Game and Fish Commission.

of caves. Eight species of Ozark plants and animals in Arkansas exist in five or fewer locations in the world, and thirteen in twenty or fewer locations. Another eighteen survive in fewer than one hundred locations. At least thirteen species of Ozark plants and animals are listed as endangered or threatened with extinction.

What old growth forests are to the Pacific Northwest, the Ozark Mountains are to midcontinental North America. The mountains represent a biological and geological continuum that stretches back prior to the formation of the continent itself. Though tamed and tainted by settlers and their sawmills, the ancient ecosystems retain their vitality and biological diversity. From upland swamps to prairies and glades, from dry pine and oak-hickory forests to moist woodlands of beech and umbrella magnolia, the Ozarks remind us of the enduring influence of the landscape on all aspects of our lives. For ten thousand years now, these rugged hills have shaped human culture more than humans have shaped them.

The Mountains Sing

"There were banjo and fiddle players everywhere you went [when I was growing up].
Many a man when the day was over, when he'd had his dinner, would sit down and play
the fiddle or the banjo for a while, or the guitar and the old organ. Those were the
instruments when I was a child. And the singing, all kinds of British ballads. I could
record two or three albums of British ballads that I learned from my folks."
—Jimmy Driftwood at his home in Timbo, Arkansas.

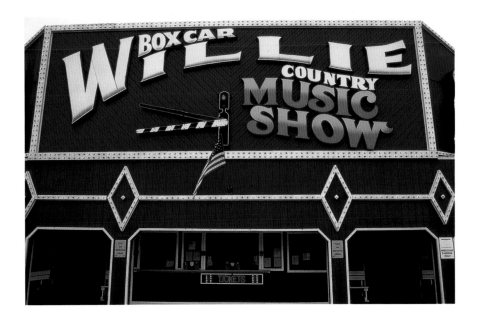

Above: Branson, Missouri. In 1987, Box Car Willie, a Grand Ole Opry star, became the first celebrity to perform in his own theater on a permanent basis in Branson. Now, more than two dozen theaters offer daily shows by nationally known celebrities.

Opposite: Mountain View, Arkansas. Musicians from around the Ozarks come to sit and pick every weekend on store porches and the courthouse square.

Mountain Music, Front-Porch Style

It is a warm Saturday afternoon around the town square in Mountain View, Arkansas, and the evening promises to be filled with fiddle, banjo, and dulcimer music accompanied by good-hearted singing. Two groups of men already have been playing for an hour or so, sitting in the shade on old kitchen chairs, folding chairs, handmade benches, and sawed-up tree trunks. Wives, children, and on-lookers tap their toes on the bare dirt of the corner lot. An older man sits on the edge of one circle and whittles a spoon from a piece of red cedar. He pulls a square of sandpaper from the pocket of his overalls and smoothes the handle.

The four musicians joke with the easy familiarity of lifelong friends and take turns choosing the next song. One man's teenage son quietly plays along, and the older men compliment and encourage him regularly. Most of the players are in their sixties, some older. One heavyset man with no teeth rolls a cigarette around his gums as he strums his guitar. After a while, a slender, middle-aged man joins the group. He is also absent of teeth and has a tanned and lined face that has seen many a plowed furrow. "How you been, Cecil?" someone asks. "Had a little heart attack last week," he says. The men shake their heads solemnly and one asks, "Can ya sing?" Cecil nods. With that settled, one of them loans Cecil a guitar and he leads the group in a song. "Cecil wrote that, you know," a woman beside me says. Several others nod in appreciation of Cecil's love ballad.

Family-style music has been synonymous with the Ozarks since the first pioneers from the Appalachians moved west with their Old World ballads and an assortment of New World instruments. Music sustained the settlers and evolved to reflect their experiences while forging a new life in the wilderness. Before paved roads stretched like tentacles into the most remote hollows, before television and rental videos held people captive in their living rooms, before the exodus from country communities to city suburbs, people in the Ozarks spent their evenings sitting on front porches rocking back and forth, visiting, and making music. During the relaxed interlude between the supper dishes and bedtime, families and friends gathered to discuss the comings and goings of the day and to play some tunes. Hands that picked cotton and shucked corn all day picked guitars, banjos, and fiddles as the shadows of the night deepened. Voices that cursed ornery mules and yelled at errant children by day, now harmonized together on gospel hymns and ballads passed down from generation to generation.

Come Saturday, farmers loaded up their wagons, then their Model Ts, and later their Chevy pick-ups, and headed into town. After the selling and shopping, they pulled out their musical instruments and sat around the courthouse square or on the gossip benches in front of the general store and traded tunes. Some towns even paved a section of the street so that players and singers and onlookers could avoid the dust and mud, and maybe even dance a jig or two—if they weren't Hard-Shell, Free Will, Primitive, Missionary, or Foot-Washing Baptists, who don't believe in dancing.

In 1922, Stone County, Arkansas, built a new courthouse on the town square in Mountain View. The maple trees grew tall and shaded the broad lawn around

"As a child, my grandmother would entertain me on the front porch of her home north of Scottsville near the Illinois Bayou. She played her harmonica and strummed her guitar at the same time. She knew all the old songs and would play the harmonica on her birthday. She lived to 102, and I credit mountain music and Ozark hardiness for that."
—John Heuston, writer, photographer, and president of the Pulaski Chapter of the Ozark Society.

Opposite: Timbo, Arkansas. Jimmy
Driftwood, whose song "The Battle of
New Orleans" launched him into
international fame as a folk singer, helped
establish the Ozark Folk Center in
Mountain View. His wife, Cleda, and the
guitar made by his Civil War–veteran
grandfather are never far from his side.

*"When I think of the Ozarks,
I think first of the trout fishing
and the music. The Ozarks are a
place where I can take my guitar
and sit and play at the Mountain
View Folk Music Festival."*

**—Jim Guy Tucker,
Governor of Arkansas.**

the ornate, native-stone structure. For years, it was the perfect place to spend Saturday, picking and singing the old tunes. But as the decades passed, the strumming faded and the only sounds accompanying the rustle of the evening breeze became the passing of a few cars on the dirt crossroads leading in and out of town.

As small communities withered, the tradition of the weekend sing-alongs began to disappear. More and more guitars and fiddles were relegated to musty closets and forgotten shelves. More and more old songs were buried in hilltop cemeteries. Pickin' and grinnin' on the town square seemed as destined to become a relic as country-store checkers and house calls from the doctor.

From the 1940s on, Mountain View merchants tried every scheme imaginable to attract tourist dollars to their impoverished county, including a national crossbow championship and a folk festival. At first, the closest paved road was forty miles away, and the town could not even afford a sewage and water system. In 1953, the blacktop reached the city limits, but city sewer and water, and the rebirth of mountain music tradition would have to wait another two decades. These accomplishments took the vision and determination of an eighth-grade teacher and an official act of the United States Congress.

Jimmy Driftwood, born James Morris in 1907, has two passions in life: music and teaching. He learned the music from his father and his grandfather, a Civil War veteran. He began teaching without formal education beyond high school. After finishing the elementary grades in the one-room schoolhouse in Mountain View and graduating from high school, Jimmy taught at Parma, a tiny community just over the mountain. He trotted seven miles to school as a student, and then twenty miles each way as a teacher. A few years later, he enrolled in Arkansas State Teachers College in Conway, now the University of Central Arkansas. He trotted two days to enroll and begin his college career.

After college, Jimmy's life as a country school teacher progressed as routinely as could be expected, with a few exceptions. He met the woman he eventually married, Cleda Azelia Johnson, when she was his sixth-grade student. When she turned nineteen and he twenty-nine, they married. Cleda shared his love for teaching and music. Jimmy first combined folk music and teaching to interest his students in his favorite subject: history. For twenty-one years he entertained students with the historical sagas he wrote, including one about the defeat of the British in New Orleans in early 1815. In 1958, he was fifty-one years old and superintendent of schools at Snowball, Arkansas, when an oral historian who collected folk music invited him to Nashville to audition some of his songs. A few months later, his "Battle of New Orleans" was a national bestseller. Jimmy retired from teaching and went on tour to sing his mountain music to audiences in the United States, Europe, and Asia. He was the first folk singer to perform in Carnegie Hall.

Jimmy's singing career stopped in 1962 as abruptly as it began. He came to realize that despite the popularity of his songs—six songs he had written were once in the top 40 at the same time—the music so dear to his heart was dying out at its roots. He returned home determined to rejuvenate the fading tradition.

His chance came when the Ozark Foothills Handicraft Guild planned a festival and asked him to invite some of his famous friends from the Nashville music

Branson, Missouri. Nick Baca, Standing Bear Buffalo Man, demonstrates his drum-making skills at the Silver Dollar City National Festival of Craftsmen.

"The thing that consistently impresses me about the Arkansas Ozarks is that they are real. The people are genuine, the music and crafts are authentic, and the scenery is unspoiled. In an increasingly plastic world, the Ozarks remain a constant haven to remind us of the things in our lives, and in our world, that are, perhaps, better off unchanged."

—Richard W. Davies, Executive Director, Arkansas Department of Parks and Tourism.

scene. Jimmy refused. He wanted to use local talent. Jimmy recalls the confrontation. "A lot of folks said, 'Hell, why would anybody come to Mountain View to hear our boys playing?' 'Because they can't hear them anywhere else!' I said." The guild finally agreed, but disappointed merchants placed bets that it would be a stretch if fifty people showed up.

Jimmy put out the word for anybody who could play to meet at the town square in Mountain View on Friday nights to get ready for the festival. The first meeting attracted six players, the next fifteen, but Jimmy had faith in his neighbors and his music. Banjos, fiddles, mandolins, and guitars that had not been tuned in years soon echoed across the town square late into the night.

The sixties was the decade of Woodstock and giant music festivals. "Of course I didn't mind going to New York and playing this kind of music and telling them about this big festival," Jimmy says. He advertised the event wherever he played, including the famous Newport Jazz Festival in Rhode Island. Finally, in the third weekend of April 1963, twenty thousand music fans came to Mountain View to the first Arkansas Folk Festival. After more than three decades, the event is still one of the premier festivals of the Ozarks.

"I'll never forget that first festival," Jimmy says. "I got an old man from back here towards Leslie that played a bagpipe to come. That night we had three shows in the school gymnasium. When it came time for him to play, he just got up and started playing as he marched to the stage, and some people got scared! Most people had never heard a bagpipe. I tell you that thing sounded like a thousand jackasses."

Branson, Missouri. The National Festival of Craftsmen at Silver Dollar City brings together artisans from across the Ozarks and the nation. Saw painter Ben Tate takes his inspiration from the hills of southern Missouri.

Within a decade, the festival grew to one hundred thousand people. Yet, Mountain View was still too impoverished to afford a water and sewage system. So, Jimmy asked Arkansas Congressman Wilbur Mills for help, and in a typically Ozarkian way, Jimmy and his friends went to Washington and played on the Capitol steps and for the Senate. They wanted federal funds to build a folk center to preserve the disappearing cultural heritage of the Ozarks. The town fathers instructed Jimmy to ask for no more than $45,000, lest he ruin their chances of getting anything. But Jimmy had a grander vision. He met with the House Ways and Means Committee and asked for $15 million.

With the help of Congressman Mills, who scratched all the political backs in Washington, Mountain View got its folk center. Of course, building a folk center that met federal standards required a municipal water and sewage system. The Economic Development Administration coughed up $2.1 million, and the Arkansas state government supplied another $1.9 million. Thanks to Jimmy Driftwood, Mountain View could finally flush its toilets.

In 1973, just ten years after Jimmy Driftwood told his friends to "go rouse the talent out of the hills," the Ozark Folk Center opened. Now, more than two decades later, the Folk Center sponsors daily programs of folk music and demonstrations of artisans making crafts in the style and with the tools of the 1920s. With the help of the Center, local artists are thriving and producing exquisite traditional crafts once threatened with extinction. Mountain View has a fine-art gallery, and roadside shops sell artisan-made products, not just tourist novelties. The Ozark Foothills Handicraft Guild has evolved into the Arkansas Craft Guild,

Branson, Missouri. Bobby Vinton is just one of the many stars from Hollywood, Las Vegas, and New York to open a theater in Branson. After spending a life on the road, the performers love having a permanent home and the creative freedom of their own theater.

with stores in five cities that offer the finest crafted items in the state. The Home Shopping Cable network even picked up a local broom maker's ware and offered it to the nation. Before the Folk Center opened, Stone County was the second poorest county in Arkansas, with 54 percent of the population on welfare. Now, less than 5 percent need public assistance.

On Friday and Saturday nights, musicians, many in dusty overalls, still gather on the Mountain View town square and at Jimmy Driftwood's Barn, a theater on the edge of town. Music lovers come from hundreds of miles to pick and grin and enjoy the magic of authentic, porch-style mountain music. The celebration of folk music and traditional crafts is in Mountain View to stay.

The Magical Music of Branson

For decades, the voice of the hills diminished from a musical celebration to a mumble, yet it refused to be silenced. Instead of dying, the music evolved again, as it had countless times in ages past, and reemerged anew in two of the most remote, rugged areas of the Ozarks. Not long after traditional mountain music experienced its renaissance in Mountain View, the hills a few miles north began to sing their own toe-tapping tunes. Pickin' and grinnin' embraced the world of high-tech audio and stage performance and evolved into a phenomenon surpassing even Jimmy Driftwood's most ambitious visions. If you join the crowds and travel to Branson, Missouri, you will find thirty-nine theaters with more than

"Many who have been lured to Branson by music have missed the region's most magnificent sights. A sizable percentage of people come just to visit the shows and never get to experience the natural beauty of the Ozarks. The town of Branson is but a tiny island of glitz and development in an ocean of otherwise unspoiled wilderness."

—Lou Schaefer, Mayor, Branson, Missouri.

fifty polished acts straight out of Las Vegas, Nashville, New York, and Hollywood.

Branson first came to the nation's attention in 1907 when Harold Bell Wright published his novel, *The Shepherd of the Hills.* Wright depicted the hardships of the 1902 drought on the self-subsisting farmers and mountain folk of the area. The book skyrocketed in popularity and became the fourth most widely read book in publishing history at that time. Tourists flocked to Branson and nearby Hollister, the closest train depot, to see the people and locale of the book. In 1913, the U.S. Army Corps of Engineers added to the area's tourism potential by impounding the White River to form Bull Shoals Lake and Lake Taneycomo. A series of dams completed in 1950 created some of the best trout fishing lakes in the nation.

By 1960, tourism in Branson was thriving enough to support two new entertainment ventures. Silver Dollar City, an old-time Ozarks village with handicraft demonstrations, opened at the site of the long-popular Marvel Cave, and an outdoor pageant based on *The Shepherd of the Hills* opened at the site of the homestead glorified in the novel. In 1967, the Presley family (no relation to Elvis), who had been performing in the Underground Theater at nearby Talking Rocks Cavern, built Branson's first music theater, a metal building with canvas seats. The next year, the Baldknobbers moved their family music show from the shores of Lake Taneycomo into town.

For the next sixteen years, the music scene grew slowly, until performers and theater owners changed almost yearly, when in 1983, Roy Clark opened the first theater associated with a well-known entertainer. In 1987, the Ozark Country

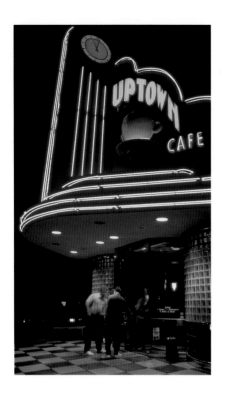

Branson, Missouri. The Uptown Cafe transports diners back to the fifties with its Art Deco architecture and old-time jukebox filled with classic hits.

Jubilee Theater opened, and the famous hobo from the Grand Ole Opry, Box Car Willie, became the first celebrity to perform on a permanent basis in his own theater. By the late 1980s, Branson was attracting nationwide publicity as major country music stars performed regularly in the theaters. In 1989, Japanese violinist and entertainer Shoji Tabuchi opened his show in a renovated theater, before building his own venue. As the decade closed, music had generated enough tourism for eleven performances to stay open through Christmas, instead of shutting down after Labor Day.

With the 1990s came an avalanche of music shows, theaters, condos, resorts, outlet malls, miniature golf and go-carts, all-you-can-eat buffets—and bumper-to-bumper traffic. Wayne Newton brought his show from Las Vegas, Anita Bryant came from Florida, and Mel Tillis, Tony Orlando, Bobby Vinton, and the Osmond family joined the stampede. By the mid-nineties, five million people a year were journeying to the once-remote hamlet to see the hottest names in music, comedy, and theater.

Despite the glitz and pizzazz of the shows and the celebrity theaters, Branson remains philosophically different from Las Vegas and other towns showcasing high-profile performers. First, every show is family oriented. Since the first music shows, performances by and for families have made Branson famous as a center for wholesome entertainment. "Branson reminds me of what America used to be like," said Bobby Vinton after he opened his theater. "It's a place where you can see any show with your family without fear of being embarrassed, and a place where you can walk down the street without fear of crime." Comedian-musician Jim Stafford agrees. "Branson is a life raft in a storm. It's America's hometown."

"We've always dreamed of this," said the Lennon Sisters, who perform at the Lawrence Welk Theater. "We can live at home and be with our friends instead of moving from hotel to hotel on tour. And fifteen members of our family perform with us at the theater."

Branson's second claim for distinction also dates back to the first family-run theaters. Since the performers own their theaters, they can write their own shows. "You can't do that in the casinos in Las Vegas," said Tony Orlando. "In Branson we can flex muscles we didn't know we had. The audience gets to see a deeper side of our creative spirit." Every joke Jim Stafford tells on stage is an immediate test of his creative genius. "All the entertainers love Branson because nobody tells you what to do with your career—except the audience."

Eddie Rabbit's show in Glen Campbell's Goodtime Theater is typical of the unusual combination of the highest level of pride and professionalism and the down-home country spirit of pickin' and grinnin' music. The production includes fireworks, laser lights, fog, giant flags unfurling on cue, and even a curtain of streaming water for Eddie's signature song, "I Love a Rainy Night." Yet between sets and after the show, Eddie mingles with the audience, poses for photos, signs autographs, and chats with people as though they were his neighbors.

"There's nothing that parallels Branson," comedian Yakov Smirnoff said. "I've traveled around the world and never seen a place where performers are as friendly and willing to meet the people. In Russia, when you address an envelope to

Branson, Missouri. The music boom has brought high-tech theaters, shopping malls, and five million visitors a year to the once sleepy Ozark town. *Photo courtesy of The Grand Village, Branson.*

someone, the country is listed first, followed by the city, then the street address and, finally, the person's name. I am proud to be in a country where the people come first."

The family-owned and-operated theaters create a phenomenon missing from the big-city entertainment scene in other parts of the country: a true sense of community among the performers. "We all have a lot of mutual respect because we've known each other for so long," said Tony Orlando. The performers have their own weekly golf league, and in the summer, each theater fields its own team in a softball tournament.

Branson exemplifies the old expression you hear in the hills that the more things change, the more they stay the same. Shows come and go, performers bring back the hits of the forties, fifties, and sixties, and highway engineers keep searching for routes to alleviate traffic. Meanwhile, standing like a sentinel overlooking the shop-till-you-drop and go-cart madness, the surrounding mountains and lakes offer a calm respite that never falters. "I never get tired of the beauty around here," said Mel Tillis. The other performers who have escaped big-city life and moved their families to Branson agree.

So far, the values and easy-going lifestyle of the Ozarks have withstood the pressures of tourism and racehorse-paced development. Branson is still proud of its small-town heritage and is determined to protect its sense of community—all the way to the bank if necessary. "I've played a lot of towns in thirty-four years, and I've never seen more magic than in Branson—and it's just starting," said Tony Orlando. "I'd stay here if I didn't have a theater. It's my utopia."

Hillbillies, Hippies, and Déjà Vu

"[A hillbilly] reduced his wants and his needs to what hard work and the land could provide. He was independent, hospitable, and proud, and these are noble characteristics in any society. Regardless of when and where 'hillbilly' originated, it ought to be interpreted in a positive rather than negative sense and worn with pride."
—Ernie Deane, 1973, from *Ozarks Country*.

Above: Searcy County, Arkansas. Before electricity and refrigerators, cellars were a necessity to the small homesteads in the Ozarks.

Opposite: Stone County, Arkansas. An underground stream emerges from Blanchard Springs Caverns and flows into Sylamore Creek. The Ozark National Forest Service offers tours of the immense caverns.

The National Geographic Society rates Arkansas State Highway 7, a National Forest Service Scenic Byway, among the top fifty scenic drives in the nation.

Arrested Time in a Semiarrested Frontier

After meandering for forty-five miles from ridgetop to ridgetop along the Winslow Escarpment, Scenic Highway 7 plummets one thousand feet to the Buffalo River. Jasper, Arkansas, population 332 and the seat and social center of Newton County, sits at the foot of the ridge. In the 1890s, the county supported a population of fifteen thousand hardy pioneers. They clear-cut the hardwood forests, milled the timber, farmed the ridgetops, and fished the river bottoms—and then left when the land had surrendered its immediate wealth. Slowly the forests rejuvenated the mountain slopes, followed by those settlers who had learned to live in harmony with the pace of the wilderness. Today, about five thousand people eke out a living in the hills and hollows of Newton County.

Living in pace with the wilderness has become an ingrained way of life in the Ozarks. Like a clock ticking sideways, time flows in a nonlinear direction in these mountains so far removed from gridlocked, four-lane highways and one-hundred-acre shopping malls. Many residents mark their working days by the sunrise and sunset instead of by clocks. In Newton County, as in much of the Ozarks, the days seem to pass like a canoe drifting on the gentle current of the Buffalo.

The time skew of the remote hollows attracts artists, writers, and people with enough money to build their own personal refuge from the soul-rending pace of society. The founder of Celestial Seasons Tea, John Hay, bought Beckmans

ST. LOUIS

PAY PHONE

TOKYO, JAPAN-6841

LITTLE ROCK-111

DALLAS - 414

NEW ORLEANS -457

HOT SPRINGS - 164

LIQUOR - 28

MEMPHIS - 248

MARSHALL-9

I-40 - 79

"Along Highway 7, as it rises as though in preparation for a descent into the valley of the Buffalo River, there are fields of view extending north to the forests of Missouri. Here one can stand as though at the center of the universe, praying that all this beauty will survive the desolating hand of mankind."

—Dee Brown, historian, author of *Bury My Heart at Wounded Knee*.

Searcy County, Arkansas. When Congress created the Buffalo National River instead of impounding it into a lake, many canoe liveries opened to supply boats to the visitors who come to float the scenic river. This directional sign at the Buffalo Outdoor Center orients canoeists to points near and far.

Leslie, Arkansas. The influence of the hippie back-to-the-land movement of the sixties and seventies is still evident in many small towns of the Ozarks. Thousands of disenchanted youth who left the big cities in those days still call the Ozarks home.

Cave near Jasper and converted it into a $2 million, five-thousand-square-foot underground home with five bedrooms, five baths, and two Jacuzzis.

The Newton County Resource Council was searching for more pragmatic ways to capitalize on the unspoiled beauty of the wilderness. The county is one of the least populated and has the lowest per capita income in the state. With 52 percent of the work force employed beyond its borders, the county desperately needed an ecologically sustainable alternative to the declining timber industry. So the Council developed a series of eco-tours to give visitors an intimate view of the mountain ridges and deep valleys they call home. Locals lead wilderness hikes, heritage tours, and photographic workshops to some of the most remote and scenic sections of the Ozarks. Besides picturesque streams and waterfalls and mountain vistas, visitors find that déjà vu comes easily along the narrow blacktop and winding dirt roads. The more you visit Newton County, the more trouble you have discerning in which decade the arrested clock of the Ozarks is ticking.

On Saturday nights in Jasper you can sip coffee with the locals in Junk & Java. Called the "Gourmet Coffee and Fine Junk Shop," it sits on the town square directly across from the courthouse. The Ozark Cafe, next door, closes early in the evening. Besides Junk & Java, the only other businesses open in town are a hippie bead store with crystals, earrings, and hundreds of little boxes of beads; a hamburger stand; and a convenience store down the street.

Junk & Java is on the cutting edge of haute cuisine in the woods. The menu lists nine types of coffee, steamers, and espresso, and a choice of eight desserts, sandwiches, and quiche. I order a slice of quiche and listen to the Nirvana album *Incesticide* playing over the sound system. Reminiscent of the art deco era, black and white tiles cover the floor in a checkered pattern. A chessboard sits ready on one table, and a quilt hanging on the wall adds a country touch to the decor.

A narrow hall leads to a back reading room with alternative newspapers and magazines. Doorways at each end of the two-table-wide dining area open into the junk store. You can buy tie-dyed shirts, incense, peace and yin and yang symbol necklaces, and books on dream interpretation and developing psychic abilities. In the sixties, we called this kind of store a head shop, but in the last decade of the twentieth century in Jasper, Arkansas, it is more politically correct to call it a junk store.

A blonde teenager with shoulder-length hair puts on a Jimmy Hendrix CD and brings my quiche and coffee. I recognize the dish as a microwaveable product from the freezer unit at Sam's Wholesale Club, which is also the origin of most of the desserts. I am sharing the six-table cafe with two men, one with three little boys and the other with a boy and girl, all drinking hot chocolate steamers and eating pastries. It is family night in Jasper, and Junk & Java is the only action in town. The closest movie is twenty miles away in Harrison, or at the relic drive-in theater fifty miles distant in Marshall.

I first met the proprietor of Junk & Java, Nancy O'Keefe, nearly ten years ago when we both lived in Austin, Texas. In an it's-a-small-world conversation, we discovered we had a mutual acquaintance in her hometown, Parthenon, Arkansas, a tiny community just down the road from Jasper. Like many Ozark natives who had aspired to escape the limitations of rural life, the pull of the Ozarks finally brought her back. But she returned with a taste for city life and exotic coffees.

So Jasper has a coffee house and junk shop out of the past, including a "lady singing the blues." By the time I finish my quiche, Mary Kay Heffron takes the stage. She wears faded blue jeans and a plaid shirt with her long hair pulled straight back. Her little girl plays in the junk shop while she tunes her guitar. Through the store window behind her I see four teenage boys playing hackysack under a streetlight on the courthouse lawn. Two fifteen-year-old girls watch from a bench and puff Camel cigarettes. Mary Kay introduces herself and launches into an antiwar ballad. I am convinced that time has come unhinged, and I have tumbled back into the sixties, when protesting youth clung to the innocent belief that ideals would eventually right the wrongs of an unjust society.

"I came to the Ozarks the way Thoreau came to Walden Pond, by way of experiment, by way of wanting to learn what I would need to know of the world that had not already been offered. Living in these woods has helped me see more clearly, I think. I have come to see each tree individually, each leaf, each bud. I have come to appreciate every sunrise as something which will never be repeated, and I have learned to slow down and be patient. I have come to understand that what I am after is as much spiritual as it is literary and musical."
—Andrea Hollander Budy, poet and author of *House Without a Dreamer.*

Autumn
by
Andrea Hollander Budy

For a week or more
the road to town grows
red, then melon, gold,
then brown. Then it's done:
one afternoon that
drunken hobo,
the wind, knocks through
taking everything
we wanted saved.
Endless as the clock,
it'll look this way for months:
gray sky banked by gray trees,
those guiltless ladies
in constant mourning,
while day-glo hunters
cock their guns.

The New Hillbillies

After the flower children and political unrest of the sixties, a back-to-the-land movement of thousands of disenchanted youth and Vietnam War protesters highlighted the seventies. Attracted by inexpensive and isolated land, many made their way into the Ozarks. In those years, I journeyed north from Houston, buying land near Clinton, Arkansas, never realizing that the twisting threads of fate would lead me all over Texas before depositing me back in the Ozarks some twenty-five years later.

Like the wave of immigrants that flooded the mountains a century ago, the new hillbillies of the 1970s "settled up" the remote hollows and valleys. They sought to get as far as they could from the warring mind sets and censuring attitudes of Middle America. But unlike their predecessors, most came with a college education and a world view that included acceptance of different cultures, values, and races.

Like many of their Appalachian predecessors, the modern back-to-the-landers came to stay. They put down roots, reared families, and lived out their ideals with as little outside interference as possible. Many pooled their money and bought land for communes. They home-schooled their children. A quarter-of-a-century later, many of those communes still exist quietly amid the unnamed dirt roads and one-store hamlets.

The first hillbillies that sought refuge in the Ozarks were called renegades. The new hillbillies are called artists and entrepreneurs and blend in with the mountains as readily as their antebellum predecessors. Both groups brought a strong sense of individualism and self-sufficiency, a new vision, a new set of skills, and a new energy to the sixty-three-million-year-old mountains. After two decades of life in the woods, a strong artist community has developed in Eureka Springs, creating world-class art and marketing it on both coasts. A new generation of folk musicians sustains the traditional mountain music. In fact, it is thriving in Mountain View, Arkansas. Middle-aged hippies operate gourmet restaurants and bakeries in their remote communities, while others write award-winning poetry and fiction. Others built small-town businesses into Fortune 500 companies. And some introduced an illegal cash crop, marijuana, whose profits from time to time infuse the economy of traditionally impoverished communities with an economic high.

As the twentieth century draws to a close, history again repeats itself. A new generation of immigrants are moving en masse to the Ozarks. Again the "semiarrested frontier" of the Ozarks is absorbing a group of Americans searching for change and opportunity. But unlike the youthful pioneers of the past, the latest wave of wanderers have already lived long and fruitful lives. They come to the hills and hollows not to exploit or escape, but to relax. Burgeoning retirement communities around the many scenic lakes of the Ozarks offer a peaceful retreat from the hectic lifestyle of the cities. While most rural areas in the heartland are declining in population and losing their traditional and historical integrity, the Ozarks maintain a strong sense of place.

Festivals of the Hills

"Large community celebrations on the Fourth of July and "Decoration Day"
(Memorial Day) were common throughout the Ozarks. There would be sack races,
baseball games, homemade ice cream, and watermelon. Attractions . . . often
included balloon ascensions, orators, circle swings, lemonade stands, the shooting
of fireworks, recitations, songs, and instrumental music."
—Phyllis Rossiter, 1992, *A Living History of the Ozarks*.

Above: Little Scotia Pond, Dent County, Missouri. The two national forests in the Ozark Mountains maintain numerous lakes, camping areas, picnicking parks, and hiking and equestrian trails. The Newton County Wildlife Association, among many other groups in the region, promotes legislation to protect environmentally sensitive areas.

Opposite: Pope County, Arkansas. The first cool nip in the air brings a pallet of rainbow hues to the forest and announces the time for fall festivals in small towns throughout the Ozarks.

Ponca Wilderness Area, Newton County, Arkansas. Kayakers and canoeists float down the Buffalo National River, once destined to be dammed. Conservation organizations such as the Newton County Wildlife Association keep diligent watch over developers, dam builders, and timber operations to prevent the exploitation that destroyed the virgin forest 100 years ago.

Forest Guardians Celebrate

As can be expected from any people living in remote, isolated homesteads, the new hillbillies, like the old-time inhabitants, enjoy a get-together and look for any excuse to socialize with their neighbors. Holiday celebrations and festivals provide the perfect opportunity. Unlike chamber of commerce events designed to attract tourists, small-town Ozark festivals bring the residents out of the hills to see each other, not strangers.

Each fall, the Newton County Wildlife Association, a grassroots activist organization dedicated to protecting the forests and streams of the Ozarks, sponsors Forest Fest in Ponca, Arkansas, a tiny community on the Buffalo River. A dozen frame homes, several kit log houses, a defunct church with a For Sale sign, a gas/convenience store, and two canoe liveries line the blacktop that cuts a sinuous path through the narrow valley. As with many historic hamlets along the Buffalo, canoe renting infuses seasonal economic life into this town.

The annual harvest celebration is in full swing when I arrive late in the afternoon. I park in the grassy ditch alongside the road, buy a soda, and proceed to mingle with the crowd. The first booth I see is sponsored by the Wildlife Association. A wolf stares from the front of the group's brochure, with the caption, "Keeping Our Eyes on the Forest." Another shows a solemn-faced man in a clear-cut holding a bumper sticker that says "Stumps Don't Lie." It would be a mistake to think that activists who are dedicated enough to their ideals to leave

"When I think of the Ozarks, I remember the day my father took me to a mountain, the place his father had taken him—the place where the Old Ones [Cherokee] wait to share their wisdom. I still go there to renew my spirit. The legacy of the Ozarks is that my sons and grandsons can go there too."
—Barbara Meyer, President, Ozark Society.

the cities and move to the woods would sit idly by while the U.S. Forest Service clear-cut, burned, bulldozed, herbicided, and pesticided the forest around them. Or that activists would turn a blind eye while the Forest Service dammed rivers, logged sensitive watersheds, and poisoned the hardwoods so only pines would grow, and then watch as the government sold the timber at below cost to lumbering companies.

True to their ideals, the county residents organized and became an outspoken, proactive voice. Appropriately for a group of people who answered the inner call, they named their newsletter the *Call of the Wild*. In addition to education, research, and development of a master plan for sustainable economic use of the forest, the association's official operational plan calls for "on the ground resistance if necessary." The Wildlife Association helps identify environmentally sensitive areas, disseminate facts, and plan and promote legislation. Members also "hike, explore, canoe, swim, camp, and just have some plain ol' fun." On this particular evening, it is evident they are here to have plain ol' fun.

Mingling with the crowd, you will see tie-dyed, ankle-length skirts; long, flowing hair (on the men); beads; peace symbols; and clusters of tents. Time flashes three decades back to the sixties. Apparently, time stopped for these back-to-the-landers the day they disappeared down rutted dirt roads into unnamed hollows. And it stopped for their children, too. You see groups of teenagers hanging out around campfires wearing layers of cottons and polyesters, patched jeans, and high-top hiking boots—mirror images of their parents' youth.

Quilting is a favorite pastime in the Ozarks. Craft shows feature demonstrations, roadside shops hang quilts for sale on fences and porches, and backyard clotheslines offer testimony to the frequent use of the traditional covering.

A scattering of booths, mostly tables beside battered pickup trucks (nothing fancy here), sell organic apples, handmade jewelry, tie-dyed clothes, goatskin drums, and high-tech solar panels for residential electricity in remote areas. I wander to the end of the grassy field and listen to a woman playing folk music on the festival's makeshift stage. She's here thanks to a grant from the Arkansas Arts Council. The folk singer sits on a stool Joan Baez style, with tie-dyed sheets tacked up for the backdrop, and strums her acoustic guitar and sings with no other accompaniment. She finishes her set and hands the stage over to a local teenage rock and roll band, which starts playing popular music from the 1970s.

My attention turns from the stage to my stomach. For food I have a choice of roasted corn, barbecued chicken, bean burritos, and falafels on pita bread, with garden fresh tomatoes and endives for condiments. A bearded man runs back and forth to a faucet to wash the plastic dinner plates as people return them. Paper plates or plastic utensils would not go over well at such an event; the garbage is divided into separate barrels for food scraps, aluminum, and trash. Newton County is dry, so there is no beer, and marijuana is also absent, even though the county is famous for its bountiful harvest. I see folks just having a good time visiting, dancing in the dark, and playing hackysack. No cops, no rowdy people, just home folks coming out of the hills to socialize and reinforce their efforts to preserve the woodlands they love. It is a night of unpretentious entertainment. It is authentic. It is a grassroots, hillbilly family-value festival, 1990s style. Some things are too good to change.

Kilts, the Caber Toss, and the Parade of Tartans

Batesville, Arkansas. Julie Stow shows a youngster at the Ozark Scottish Festival how to weave a basket from strips of white oak. Ozark artisans have turned the utilitarian craft of basket weaving into a fine art form.

Just as the first-generation inhabitants of the hills celebrated their new homeland, residents who trace their descendants back to antebellum immigrants honor their lineage. Lyon College in Batesville, Arkansas, hosts the annual Ozark Scottish Festival and Highlands Games each spring. Batesville, the oldest town in Arkansas still in existence, traces its roots back to 1804 when a Scottish settler named McFarland built a log house on the White River. Presbyterians founded the liberal arts school in 1872. The college celebrates its roots with a Scottish Heritage Program and a Scottish Arts Company, which perform with pipers, harpists, drummers, and dancers.

I hear bagpipes echoing across the rolling campus as I approach the festival area. Across a small creek, scattered clusters of performers rehearse in the shade of ancient oak trees. Gaily colored tents circle an open field, and kilt-clad people mill about eating Scottish meat pies and bread. Various clans have booths decorated with their coat of arms and tartan plaids. The dancing competition is in full swing on stage, with young girls pirouetting to the Highland Fling and the Scottish Lilt.

I have never seen so much plaid in all my life. Caps, knee socks, dresses, ties, kilts, and flags sport the tartan patterns—all in 100 percent worsted wool. Boys wearing kilts along with their fashion-conscious grade school wardrobe (tee shirts

Batesville, Arkansas. Children at the Ozark Scottish Festival test their strength at tossing the sheaf, a hay-filled burlap sack, over a bar. In addition to athletic games, the ethnic celebration features dancing, music, food, and crafts.

"I've lived and worked in the Ozarks for more than seven years and the beauty of the hillsides and the warmth of the people amaze me.
**—John D. Linahan,
Superintendent,
Buffalo National River**

and unlaced, black high-tops) stand in line for the kid's version of the adult contests. A man with a thick Scottish accent directs me to the Highland games area where the adults are competing.

Like the games at pioneer folk festivals, Scottish sports trace their origin to the common skills needed to work a farm. Men using a three-pronged pitch fork toss a sixteen-pound sheaf of straw over a crossbar. The competitors display enough strength to toss considerable hay into a barn loft as they attempt to best the twenty-six-foot, four-inch record. The rolling pin toss for women, if combined with sufficient accuracy, would have great practical value for dealing with husbands who nip the bottle too much. The origin of the caber toss, how far you can throw a small telephone pole, is a bit more obscure to me. But as a test of strength, this activity would certainly indicate who to invite to the next barn raising. In another corner of the festival grounds, border collies demonstrate their sheep-herding skills.

Soon after lunch, the crowd gathers around the open field for the Parade of Tartans, an official recognition of each family, or clan, represented at the festival.

The blast of 100 bagpipes blows through the gathering like a cyclone as the procession marches past. Each clan proudly carries its tartan colors and insignia as it circles the field.

Hundreds of people have gathered today from the Ozark region and surrounding states in unabashed pride of their ethnic heritage. How refreshing to see ethnicity celebrated instead of denied, or worse yet, suppressed. What better example of how the freedom to express our cultural diversity enriches the life experience of us all. From Appalachian hillbillies to Scottish Highlanders, from displaced Native Americans to slaves, from French to Spanish and finally to English, the genealogy of many cultures is etched in the unnamed cemeteries of the Ozarks. But historically, the rugged mountains have never been able to accept more than one culture at a time. Many Ozark counties did not even have schools for African-Americans before 1965. But now as multiculturalism becomes an accepted way of life and as industries relocate to the Ozarks and bring in ethnic workers, the white monoculture, which has dominated the Ozarks since the Native Americans were driven out 150 years ago, may finally be diversifying.

As the twentieth century fades into history, a new influence is developing in the northwest corner of Arkansas. The year 1994 saw the first Hispanic newspaper, cable television channel, and radio station in the Fayetteville area. The rapidly increasing population of Mexican-American poultry and agricultural workers has become a recognized element of the community. Maybe someday *Cinco de Mayo* will take its place alongside the many celebrations that add such a rich and distinct flavor to the rural communities of the Ozarks.

Batesville, Arkansas. The Parade of Tartans, a marching band of bagpipes representing the Scottish families that settled the Ozarks, highlights the Ozark Scottish Festival, hosted each spring by Lyon College.

53

A Country Store in a Worldwide Market

"Stores were located wherever they could most profitably serve the most people . . . by necessity there was a store every few miles to which customers walked, rode horseback, or drove a buggy or wagon. A very few, in some of the more remote areas, still operate; often the storekeeper is quite elderly and is a fund of information about the neighborhood and its history."
—Phyllis Rossiter, 1992, *A Living History of the Ozarks*.

Above: Eureka Springs, Arkansas. Joe Harp chats with a customer outside his family's store. His father, Albert, born in 1901, operates the store, which has been in the family since 1885.

Opposite: Mountain View, Arkansas. Shoppers take time for a game of checkers on the porch of Mellon's Country Store. Small stores dot the Ozarks and often serve as social gathering points, as well as places to buy goods.

Eureka Springs, Arkansas. The old "Flat Iron" Building stands like a sentinel over the historic downtown district. The town once attracted visitors to its therapeutic baths, but now tourists come to see the Victorian architecture.

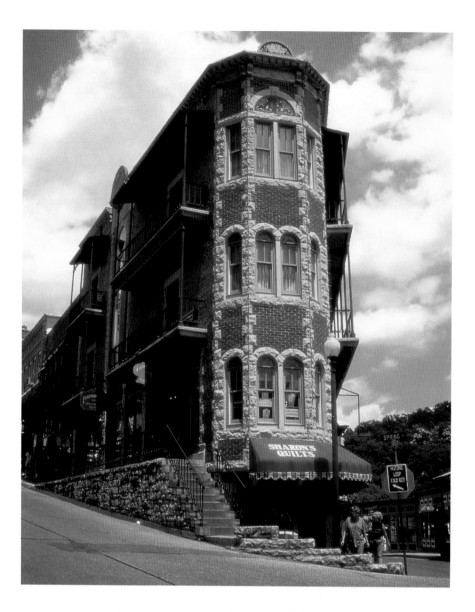

"Finally, . . . the country store gave way to the shopping center. One old storekeeper in northern Arkansas summed up the problems. . . . 'The thing that really tore the fabric of it was the car . . . good roads, cars, and rural routes put me out of business.'"
—**Nancy McDonough, 1975, *Garden Sass: A Catalog of Arkansas Folkways.***

Groceries with a History

In an effort to attract tourist dollars, the state of Arkansas recently changed its motto from "The Land of Opportunity" to "The Natural State." Yet many entrepreneurs still find that an area rich in natural resources with only 2.5 million inhabitants is indeed the land of opportunity. The impoverished economy of the Ozarks translates into an abundance of cheap labor and low operating expenses. In less than half a century, the country store, with a marketing area once measured by the roundtrip distance a wagon could travel in a day, has evolved into retail outlets that tap the world market. Ironically, the Ozarks, remote and isolated from the financial centers of the nation, have spawned some of the largest and wealthiest entrepreneurs in the history of free enterprise.

Sam Walton, founder of the discount store empire that made him the richest man in the world, began with one small store in Bentonville, Arkansas. In the beginning, he searched for twenty people to invest $5,000 each, but many thought he was a bad business risk. In 1995, Wal-Mart posted $82.5 billion in sales with more than two thousand stores, making it the largest retailer in the nation and probably the world. Patti Upton, a former Miss Arkansas and homemaker "with a black belt in shopping," started mixing flower petals and aromatic oils in her kitchen in Heber Springs. She turned her good business "scents" into a $100-million-a-year business, Aromatique. Anyone traveling the interstates is familiar with the yellow trailers of J. B. Hunt Transport Company. Hunt, owner of one of the largest trucking concerns in the nation, rolled his first truck out of Lowell, Arkansas, near Fayetteville, to transport surplus hulls from rice mills in southern Arkansas to chicken farmers in the Ozarks. Don Tyson, with a personal wealth valued at $800 million, started Tyson Chicken in Springdale, Arkansas, just south of Lowell. Tyson, the nation's largest poultry producer, earned $5.1 billion in revenues in 1994. Down the road in Rogers, Hudson Foods, the sixth-largest poultry producer in the country, grossed $1.04 billion. Chicken houses in Washington and Benton counties alone feed twenty-four million chickens a month.

However, not all businesses rate their success in the millions they make. The sign on a storefront in Eureka Springs, Arkansas, says "Harp's Grocery, Oldest Store in Town, Est. 1885." A jingling bell on the door announces my entrance and hints of a time when store owners knew customers by their first names and carried accounts for most. The first thing you will see when you step inside Harp's Grocery is a rack loaded with Twinkies and white bread. The store contains about as much merchandise as a 7-Eleven, but you'll see at a glance that this is no ordinary convenience store. Shelves stretch the length of the narrow room and reach almost to the fifteen-foot-high ceiling. Racks of snack food surround a center island with the cash register, and a meat and cheese case filled with antique dolls occupies the rear.

Unlike the hundreds of other shops in Eureka Springs' picturesque shopping district, Harp's Grocery sells no tee shirts, no machine-made quilts, no corn husk dolls, and no made-in-Asia "Ozark" souvenirs. Harp's started selling groceries 110 years ago, and food items still line the original shelves. I see a bearded, gray-haired man in the rear peeling plastic wrap from a slice of processed cheese. He looks almost as old as the worn wooden floors. I ask him if he is the proprietor. He nods yes between bites.

Albert Harp munches his cheese snack beside a table covered with antique kitchen appliances and implements from an era when things were built to last several lifetimes. From his vantage point in the back of the store, he can see memorabilia accumulated during the ninety years of his lifetime. Sandwiched between the canned goods are enough historic relics to fill a museum. I move aside a box of generic hot chocolate and look at a photo of Albert's wife surrounded by hundreds of dolls. Zoe's collection, valued at $100,000 when she died, fills the store next door, which is no longer open to the public.

"I knew Zoe all my life," Albert says. "We grew up as neighbors and married when we were eighteen." They were both born in 1904, just twenty-five years after the town was founded. Zoe died in 1992, after seventy years of marriage.

Albert and Zoe did not start out to be store owners. Music was their family passion and later became the career of their only child, Joe. Along with Zoe's sister and other family members, the couple performed the Ozark Family Hill Folks Musical and Comedy Review in Eureka Springs' Basin Park for thirty-

Every town has its café; you can always get an ice-cold drink on a steamy, summer day. The small-town businesses of the Ozarks have survived the great changes to the region and retain the true character of the mountains.

Eureka Springs, Arkansas. The Fuller House, circa 1891, is one of the dozens of Victorian houses converted into bed and breakfasts. The quaint houses and hillside streets preserve the city's turn-of-the-century charm.

"My home was between two streams that flowed in opposite directions, the Little Red River flowing east into the White River and Cadron Creek flowing west into the Arkansas River. After a heavy rain, all traffic stopped at these streams. Wildlife was special to me. I learned to identify birds and their calls from the color picture-cards of songbirds that came in boxes of Arm and Hammer baking soda."
—Dr. Roy Thomas, author, folklorest

seven years. Meanwhile, Zoe's sister and her husband sold Albert and Zoe the family store forty-five years ago, and the Harps continued on at the store after their musical careers ended.

As the years passed, the collection of family heirlooms began to fill the top shelves and spread down into the merchandise. Now, toys and household items as old as Albert himself reach toward the ceiling from the top shelf and mingle below with mops, Bugles, and canned beans. I ask about a ceramic teepee. "It was a bank. An Indian pulled a frog out of the water when you dropped in a coin," Albert says. I also look over flat irons, ceramic figurines, a metal bulldog, and several items of undetermined intention. Albert finishes his snack and returns to his place at the cash register. I ask him about a framed picture of Carry Nation, the turn-of-the-century temperance activist, leaning against a shelf of canned tomatoes. "Zoe was the last living member of Carry Nation's Sunday school class," Albert tells me.

58

Looking past cans of creamed corn and green beans, I find a photo of a mustached young man in a vintage fireman's uniform. Eureka Springs is a town filled with old-time photo studios where tourists pose in period costumes, but this is the real thing. The man is Zoe's father, who later became the chief of police, a post which included the duty of keeping the famous temperance leader from disturbing local saloons. Another photo depicts a rowdy group of vigilantes brandishing pistols while sitting on a Model A with flat tires. "They just shot two bank robbers and wounded the driver," Albert says. The bandits tried to hire Albert to drive for them without divulging their intentions. Luckily, he refused.

A customer comes in and takes a six-pack of cold drinks from the refrigerator in the back. A hand-lettered sign says, "Sodas, 50¢." Soft drinks cost seventy-five cents to a dollar in the rest of this tourist town. Albert rings up the sale on a cash register that itself belongs in a museum and chats briefly with the man, a regular customer. Two tourists wander in and gaze at the odd assortment of merchandise and antiques. They ask about the dolls in the meat cooler, then leave without buying anything.

Albert Harp and Sam Walton, founder of Wal-Mart, both began with small stores in rural towns in Arkansas, but the similarity ends there. While Walton went on to become the world's largest merchandiser, Albert refuses to sell the most interesting items in his store—the antiques. He has also repeatedly turned down offers to sell the store, and he will not retire. "I'll retire the day they take me to the cemetery," he says.

On weekends, Albert's only son, Joe, comes in to help. Joe, who is sixty-seven, also has only one son. The Harp family has gone 114 years without a female descendant. Joe wants to keep the store open when Albert cannot run it anymore, but he already has plenty to keep him busy. The Harps own twelve rental houses, three stores, and a 100-acre farm outside of town. "I'll try to find a couple that can work here and live upstairs," he says.

I ask Albert if I can photograph him in front of the shelves of antiques and canned goods. He takes out his pocket comb and runs it through his thick white hair several times and obliges me. I stand on top of the ice cream freezer to get a view of the whole store. Despite my wide-angle lens, I know I can capture only a 1/60th-of-a-second glimpse of Albert's lifetime in the store. He has seen airplanes evolve into space shuttles, telegraphs into televisions, and crank telephones into the information superhighway. Harp's Grocery has survived two world wars, the Depression, fast food, and wholesale outlet malls. I sense a certain stability in this eclectic mix of canned goods, snack foods, and family heirlooms.

Every morning at 8 A.M., seven days a week, Albert Harp comes down from his apartment above the store and unlocks the front door, as he has for the last forty-five years. In its 110-year history, the grocery has closed only once—the week Zoe died. Albert sits behind his register and rings up one-dollar sales and chats with the regulars until closing time at 6 P.M. Sam Walton would have been aghast at the store's low volume, but with a record of more than a century of service, the Harp family might have a few lessons for the discount merchandisers of the world.

A rusty, thirty-cents-a-gallon gas pump at an abandoned station reflects how fast times can change, even in the once-remote Ozarks. But as Albert Harp could testify, many things stay the same.

Gourmet Hubcaps
and Flemish Bread

*"Lois went out and picked a batch of tender young [poke greens] . . . and parboiled
them for about 15 minutes. She poured off the water from the greens and put them in
a pot with the ham hock, added a little salt, and let them cook slowly for an hour. . . .
I split a couple of cornbread sticks and soaked the sticks with the pot likker.
I wish I could describe exactly how delicious the combination of poke greens,
pot likker, and cornbread really was."*
—Ernie Deane from *Ozarks Country*, 1972.

Above: Gilbert, Arkansas. Whether traveling by canoe or car, the Riverside Kitchen is a
must-stop for delicious, country-cooked victuals.

Opposite: The Buffalo National River attracts thousands of canoeists each year, which
boosts the economy of many small towns along the river.

The Riverside Kitchen and Bakery

The only paved road out of Gilbert, Arkansas, population forty-three, is also the only one that comes in. Not many people pass through, except floaters. Gilbert, located at a bend in the Buffalo National River, may be the only town where more visitors arrive via canoes than cars. But following the paved roads, TV dish antennas, and fax machines, a little cafe with first-class food has infiltrated this remote settlement.

Sherry Kessler moved to Gilbert from Little Rock four years ago and converted an old farmhouse into the Riverside Kitchen and Bakery. She tried a bed and breakfast venture, but decided to stick with what she loves best: cooking. Sherry is no stranger to the restaurant business. Her Little Rock cafe, Hungry's, served generous amounts of what many considered the best home-cooked food in the state. But living in downtown Little Rock proved to be too much of a strain on her family. "My eight-year-old daughter didn't even have a place to ride her bicycle. And I wanted to get her in a small-town school. The restaurant is seasonal here, so I can spend five months of the year with her."

But the other seven months take ninety hours a week from Sherry and her parents. "Mama's sixty-five, but she can run circles around any twenty-three-year-old waitress," Sherry says. "She waits the tables and works right beside me in the kitchen. Daddy barbecues the ribs, brisket, and chicken, and takes care of the maintenance."

Wondering how Riverside Kitchen cuisine compares with Hungry's reputation, I turn off Highway 65 and take the winding three-mile trek to Gilbert. It is still early in the morning and about half of the six tables are occupied with overall-clad clientele. No one seems in a hurry to leave. Rough-cut, oak planks cover the wall in an artistically rustic manner, supporting framed awards honoring Hungry's "Best Plate Lunch in the State" for five years in a row, along with a four-foot-long green alligator.

The breakfast menu lists "rooster bullets" (eggs, sausage, biscuits), "Aunt Mary's Special" (eggs, sausage, hash browns, grits, biscuits, and gravy), and "'57 hub-caps," among other specialties of the house. I order a short stack of hubcaps and get two hotcakes guaranteed to fill the hungriest travelers, whether they've traveled by car or canoe.

Before long, all of the tables fill with locals and rangers from the National River office across the Buffalo. A light-hearted chatter fills the cafe like the conversation around a dining room table, as Thurma Brigger, who everyone calls Mama, keeps the coffee cups brimming.

The immaculate condition of Gilbert's houses and white community building is something to be admired. None are the derelict fixer-uppers common to many communities whose glory days have passed. "How do the townspeople manage to keep all the houses in such good condition?" I ask during a lull in the Riverside Kitchen conversation. A man looks up as he sips his coffee. "Pride's cheap," he says.

As I eat my pancakes and chat with the regulars, I see that the town pride also includes the way the regulars relate to a man with Down's syndrome. He sits with

Leslie, Arkansas. David Lower supplies the Ozarks with authentic, Flemish Desem bread from his Serenity Farms Bakery. Leslie once was a booming sawmill town with 10,000 residents and the largest oak-barrel mill in the nation; now about 480 people call the town home.

a friend, sipping coffee and joking with everyone in the cafe. Unlike cities where people become numbers, tiny Gilbert acknowledges and respects all its citizens.

A thirtysomething woman comes in with a clothing catalog and orders biscuits and gravy. After thumbing through the wish book while waiting for her order, she asks a table of men if anyone in town has a backhoe for hire. One man mentions a name. "Tell him to stop the next time he's passing by," she says. Then she adds, "If I can't get it done soon, I'll rent a Ditch-Witch and do it myself." She appears self-sufficient enough to do her own work, but savvy enough to network with the community. In a small town, everybody shares information to help their neighbors.

As the morning wears toward noon, the regulars drift away like canoes on a lazy river. Mama brings out a coconut cream pie covered with a mountain of meringue and puts it in the dessert cooler. She adamantly refuses to cut me a piece till it "sets up." A lady finishes her breakfast and leaves, but not before buying me the last homemade sweet roll in the box by the cash register. "It's not pie, but it'll go good with your coffee," she says with a wink.

I visit Sherry in the kitchen before I leave. Between breakfast orders, she chops okra and peels potatoes for lunch. The lunch menu lists thirty types of sandwiches, plus soups, salads, and veggies. In addition to beef, ham, shrimp, catfish, chicken, and smoked sausage Po' boys, lunch includes six variations of Sherry's famous cheeseburger. Mexrittas, a south-of-the-border invention similar to a burrito, is on for supper. Sherry may not exactly add haute to hillbilly cuisine, but she definitely adds the Riverside Kitchen to the map of the tasty victuals of the Ozarks.

When Less Means More

Leslie, Arkansas, a small town about midway between Clinton and Marshall, hides another surprise typical of the Ozarks, but atypical of its hillbilly image. The Serenity Farms Bakery practices a thousand-year-old technique of breadbaking in this hamlet. As baker David Lower pours wheat berries into his stone mill, I imagine ancient societies grinding their own flour, mixing it with water and sea salt, and baking it in a stone oven. David Lower follows those exact steps and uses the same ingredients. No dough conditioners, no preservatives, not even any baker's yeast, just three simple ingredients. And it works.

Finding the bakery in Leslie is easy. Finding anything in Leslie is easy. Just stand at the main intersection and look around. At the end of the block you will see the old Farmer's Bank Building, circa 1907, which now houses the hearth of the Serenity Farms Bakery. The red-brick edifice with its white-trimmed, arching, loaf-shaped windows and neat flower boxes is the perfect setting for the bakery. Resembling a miniature building itself, the massive brick oven occupies most of the inside space.

Like bakers of the past, David builds a wood fire in his oven on bread days. The interior reaches one thousand degrees Fahrenheit before the wood burns to ashes. David rakes out the residue and scrubs the bricks clean, then seals the oven and waits for the heat to distribute evenly throughout the bricks. Unlike primitive bakers, David knows exactly when to start cooking. He monitors the temperature with five high-tech digital probes. When the oven reaches 420–430°, he places the loaves directly on the bricks.

Leslie may seem an unlikely place to find world-class baked goods, but the town has not always been so inconspicuous. One hundred years ago, stave mills supported ten thousand residents. Wagons lined the streets with oak timber waiting to be milled. At peak production, the town produced 4,500 oaken barrels a day. When the forests surrendered the last oak, the mills closed and the workers moved on. Today, only 446 people remain. Providentially, tiny Leslie is where David Lower decided to turn his lifelong love into reality.

David worked in a natural-food store and bakery in Washington, D.C., before joining the back-to-the-land movement of the 1970s. He followed his Native American ancestry (he is one-fourth Cherokee) all the way back to the Ozarks and settled in Chimes, near Leslie. A degree in English literature did not help much in finding a job in a community so small it is not listed on the official state highway map, so David worked carpentry and operated a tree-planting business in the national forest. His wife, Chris, studied nursing and schooled their two children at home.

Then, one hot August day, David ventured into the bakery for his weekly supply of bread. "I've always been a bread freak. When the previous owner offered to sell, I couldn't resist," he says, his blue eyes sparkling proudly below his white chef's hat. "Only about ten other bakeries in the nation make authentic Flemish Desem bread."

Desem bread owes its to-kill-for flavor more to what it lacks than to its three basic ingredients. It has no yeast. It relies on a sourdough for leavening, but not

Leslie, Arkansas. Everybody enjoys a stop in the small-town cafes throughout the Ozarks.

the yeast-based sourdough in the San Francisco or Alaskan varieties. Desem leavening comes from the natural bacteria present on organically grown wheat. David's starter culture originated in Belgium, and the few bakers who share it guard it closely. "I had to promise not to give it to anyone," he explains. David also painstakingly protects the culture from airborne contamination. The starter is never exposed to air and no yeast (or anything containing yeast) is allowed inside the bakery.

Serenity Farm's bread is a godsend for people who react adversely to yeast or artificial additives. For comparison, I checked a loaf of Colonial Stone Ground Wheat bread. Of the thirty-one ingredients, stone ground wheat came in third behind enriched flour, which itself included six ingredients. Some white bread on the shelf even contained soybean-hull fiber.

While commercial bread may contain more ingredients from a chemist's lab than from a farmer's land, Serenity Farms relies solely on the robust flavor of freshly milled organic wheat. David grinds each day's flour in a stone mill from Austria. After mixing in the starter and French sea salt, he kneads the mixture in a heavy-duty machine imported from France. Then he wraps each loaf in baker's linen. He spent $2,000 on imported linen, but a tight wrap is part of the secret. According to David, wrapping the loaf slows down growth and makes the bacteria work harder.

If you think baking bread at home requires as much art as skill, you should visit David on baking days. He prepares up to seventy loaves. A smile curls from beneath his mustache as he explains, "The barometric pressure and temperature

Leslie, Arkansas. Whittlers' benches, with shavings on the ground and a complimentary wood box nearby, are still a fixture in many small Ozark towns. This bench is just down the block from David Lower's bakery.

affect the rate and amount of rising. In the summer I have to use ice water to slow down the process. Each run is different. That's the challenge that makes baking interesting. This isn't an assembly-line production."

David keeps a busy schedule baking five kinds of gourmet bread, as well as baguettes, long, crusty French loaves; apple-, fig-, and almond-filled loaves; and garlic-herb and tomato-olive focaccia, a round, Italian flat bread. In addition to his 100 percent whole wheat bread, he turns out loaves of French hearth bread, light wheat, walnut-raisin, and European rye breads. Most of his business is over the counter, but he does ship to stores from Tennessee to Washington, D.C.

The bakery's walk-in customers even get treats besides the delicious bread. David sells homegrown Yukon gold potatoes and garlic from his three-acre, organic garden. But most of all, visitors can sit and drink the gourmet coffee David serves his customers, feel the heat radiating from the massive oven, and smell the incomparable aroma of baking bread.

Art from the Flames

"My sculpture is about the power of Ozark materials. Resting and rushing water, ancient limestone, stately cedars are all discovered in the final product. The Ozarks speak of rebirth, new life after fire or flood, and that continuum inspires a daily greeting to my valley: 'Good morning world!'"
—Pat Musick, artist.

Above: Mountain View, Arkansas. A welder puts the finishing touches on wrought iron furniture at the Stone County Iron Works. National magazines and catalogs regularly feature the company's products on their covers. *Photo © by Camera Works, Inc.*

Opposite: Mountain View, Arkansas. David Mathews learned blacksmithing at the Ozark Folk Center and started a furniture business in an old service station. Now, Stone County Iron Works is the largest blacksmith shop in the nation, in terms of production, and is on the Fortune 500 list. *Photo © by Camera Works, Inc.*

Fragile Creations

You cannot help but feel a bit clumsy in Ed Pennebaker's studio. With delicate glassware covering tables and shelves from floor to ceiling, this is not a place for small children or adults carrying large camera bags. Besides, the magic of the place tempts the child within to touch everything within reach. The brilliant colors of fish-shaped perfume bottles, ribbed vases, rose-colored flasks, and teardrop ornaments flash in the sunlight streaming through the windows.

The array of glass bottles, pitchers, bowls, and other functional and decorative items reminds me of my Great Aunt Addy's untouchable collection of antique glass. But Ed does not collect glassware; he makes it. He turns the pure quartz sand mined in nearby Guion, Arkansas, twelve miles from Mountain View, into objects of exquisite beauty.

Humans began shaping obsidian and other naturally occurring glass at least a million years ago. Then some five thousand years ago, the Mesopotamians (modern-day Iraqis) discovered the secret of producing the versatile substance. Mix sand, soda (chalk), and lime (ashes), heat it to over 2,000° F, and presto! you have glass. The Romans developed the craft of glassblowing in 50 B.C. and set civilization on a path toward yet undiscovered uses of glass.

Today, Ed uses the same basic techniques and tool designs employed by the ancient Romans. Once a week, he heats his propane furnace to 2,300°F and melts 100 pounds of sand into a molten soup. He adds various metal oxides to create the colors he desires. Then he swirls his pipe into the fiery mixture and extracts it with a glob on the end. From that point on, no coffee breaks are permitted.

"Blowing glass is pretty intense," Ed says. "Once you start a piece, you can't stop until it's finished. The glass stays workable for about one minute, then it has to be reheated." Ed keeps up a shaping-heating-shaping pace for about five hours a day, then spends the afternoon packing and shipping.

Ed first sampled the art of glassmaking while in high school. He developed his skills at the historical Hale Farm and Village in Bath, Ohio. On a motorcycle trip with his parents, he discovered the beauty of the Ozarks, and in 1985, bought a studio in Salem, Arkansas. Recently he moved to his present location in the woods of Carroll County, at the end of a rutted, two-mile-long dirt road.

I follow his explicit directions and finally reach his house. Glass bobbles hang from the front porch and decorate the flower gardens. Apparently, I am at the right place. Ed's spacious house with expansive windows and rough-hewn beams stands atop a ridge overlooking the tiny community of Osage. A path leads from the road to his studio and then beyond to hiking paths that wind through the forest.

"Living in the Ozarks helps me relax," he says. "Working seven days a week wears you out. So being close to nature and away from everything is important. I like living alone."

Ed specializes in museum-quality reproductions of early nineteenth-century glassware and markets his work primarily through museum shops. He meticulously documents each style, noting its origin and use. He shows me his repro-

Mountain View, Arkansas. Don Mellon operates a country store. He also sings, while playing guitar and the spoons, on his latest recording "Don & Doug On Tour." Commerce and art go hand-in-hand in the Ozarks.

"It took us awhile to find our retreat above Ozone on top of Moonhull Mountain . . . Nature became my teacher also, and after a short while in Moonfields, I started to pile stones into silent guardians of the woods, then to assemble the primordial rocks, the hard woods, steel and bronze into fifteen-foot tall sculptures meant to be humble tributes to the beauty and strength of my new surroundings. Hopefully, time will continue to be kind to these ancient mountains that soothe the souls of the artists and the few visitors who seek beauty and peace in nature."

—Benini, artist

duction of a globe-shaped whiskey jug originally produced in Ohio between 1815 and 1850. His pattern for a teal-green, swirled bottle dates from 1824 to 1832 in Kent, Ohio. He recently began producing one-and-one-half-inch marbles with swirls of colors. I pick up one of the miniature crystal balls and feel as if I am holding a captured rainbow.

Then Ed shows me a photograph of himself with President Clinton and the First Lady. Ed was one of sixty artisans chosen to contribute a piece to the permanent collection of American crafts at the White House. He created a replica antique sugar bowl for the occasion.

After five millennia of utilitarian service, glass has finally been recognized as a fine-art medium. Beginning with the studio art-glass movement in the 1960s, glassblowing made the crossover from craft shows to gallery exhibits. The world's leading museums and galleries now display collections of glass art. Ed's decanters, marbles, and sugar bowls capture the beauty and creative spirit of the artisan's soul, and transmit it to the viewer. To me that is art at its finest.

Iron Man of the Ozarks

In 1973, David Mathews was a nineteen-year-old idealist. Like many teenagers in the back-to-the-land movement, David dropped out of an Alabama college and hit the road in his Volkswagen microbus. His goal was simple. He wanted to forge a living out of the backwoods of the Ozarks far from the mind-set of middle-class America. At the time, he had no intention of becoming a blacksmith, though he might have considered the idea. In his wildest dreams, David did not see himself building a one-man business into the largest blacksmith shop in the nation, with annual sales in the millions of dollars.

Stone County Iron Works creates a complete line of ornate furniture, such as this prototype design for a wine rack. *Photo © by Camera Works, Inc.*

David and his pregnant wife bought forty acres of land in Stone County near Mountain View, Arkansas. His homestead was remote, and did not have running water or electricity. True to his backwoodsy philosophy, David preferred the barter system to money; but even in the Ozarks, he needed some cash. Folklore had intrigued him since his days as a Boy Scout, so he hired on at the Ozark Folk Center. He mowed grass, pulled weeds, cleaned restrooms, and eventually joined an apprenticeship program to learn the disappearing art of blacksmithing.

David had always enjoyed hard, physical work. As an apprentice blacksmith, he discovered he loved pounding a white-hot bar of iron and shaping it into a functional object. He was fascinated by the simple beauty of iron furniture. But most of all, he loved creating an object that combined craftsmanship and art into a lasting piece of work. From the sparks of his sledge, David forged an enduring vision, not of money, but of creating something he believed the world needed.

After several days of phoning, I finally catch up with David in his small upstairs office in his production plant. In ten minutes he is leaving for a trade show in Atlanta. Plaques hang on the wall honoring him as the outstanding small businessman in Arkansas for 1990 and as the second runner-up for outstanding small businessman in the nation. Framed covers of national magazines and catalogs showcase his products.

Twenty years ago, David started smithing on his farm with a five-kilowatt generator for electricity. In 1979, he moved his forge and anvil to an abandoned service station in Mountain View. In the 1980s, he incorporated Stone County Iron Works with seven employees. By 1990, *Inc.* magazine listed the company as one of the five hundred fastest growing businesses in the nation. Despite the phenomenal growth and success of his business, David never lost his original vision.

David comes from behind his desk and pulls up a chair beside me so we are chatting almost knee to knee. He explains his vision, not like a man with a rehearsed script, but like a man sharing the secret location of his favorite fishing hole with a new friend.

"The world needs products that express both craft and timeless quality," he says. "We live in a post-industrial era where craft has lost its meaning. The world needs products that exemplify the old crafts to keep us from forgetting our roots. A piece that is truly a work of craft becomes more than what it is. It becomes part of the family and is passed down from generation to generation. Our furniture has set the standard for the furniture industry."

Every bedframe, lamp, fireplace tool, and even the smallest candleholder produced by Stone County Iron Works is hand forged, and each of the eighty blacksmiths has the same pride in his craftsmanship as the small-town smithies of the past. Pounding white-hot iron over a blazing forge takes a special type of person. Blacksmithing selects workers powerful of mind and will, as well as body. "Most of my employees would be considered outlaws of society," David says. "Most American workers don't participate fully with management. Blacksmiths want control over their lives, and their jobs. I knew that to succeed I had to break the us-against-them mentality."

Stone County Iron Works has two hundred workers, but no foremen, no supervisors, and no hierarchy of management. "With top-down management, the employees do what the boss says," David explains. "We have self-directed teams with the freedom to choose their own production methods. We don't do assembly-line work. Each blacksmith rotates jobs, so they all become complete craftsmen."

David is not on the production line anymore, but he still does most of the design for his expanding line of products. Then he gives it to a team and lets them decide the best way to mass produce it. The end product is a work of art, as well as a functional item. "The workers know that what they do impacts everybody. We have a bonus structure similar to a profit-sharing system. The profits the company makes translate directly into a better quality of life for all."

David began by selling his wares at craft shows and fairs, then eventually moved exclusively into the wholesale market. Neiman Marcus and Bloomingdales have featured his ornate bed frames on the covers of their catalogs, and practically every national home and furnishings magazine has used his products for cover illustrations. His sales representatives cover every state in the nation, as well as Canada, France, and Japan. Stone County Iron Works is one of the few black-smith shops with large enough production to supply the mass retail outlets.

With the largest blacksmith shop in the nation, David Mathews has come a long way since he dropped out of college. He has helped perpetuate a disappearing craft, and three presidents have awarded him for his efforts. "Governor George Wallace of Alabama even shook my hand," he says with a grin. "He had a piece of fried chicken in his other hand."

Just then, a man sticks his head in the door and announce it is time to leave for Atlanta. David apologizes and grabs his briefcase. Getting serious, he sums up the secret to his success in one simple statement: "You have to have an unyielding vision and the tenacity to see it through."

Somehow I am not surprised at David's formula. It sounds remarkably similar to the process of taking a cold iron bar and using fire, hammer, and brute strength to reveal its hidden beauty. But then, David Mathews is a blacksmith first and a businessman second.

Mountain View, Arkansas. The Case Building, on the northwestern corner opposite the courthouse, first opened its doors in 1929 as a car dealership. It supplied the county with Fords for almost fifty years. Since 1989, the building has been the retail outlet for Stone County Iron Works. *Photo © by Camera Works, Inc.*

Saving the Buffalo River

"On my son's 12th birthday, I took him hiking to a bluff high above an Ozark Valley. I hid a cake in my backpack and surprised him for lunch. After we ate, I apologized for not having much of a party. He said, 'Mom, this was the best birthday I could ever have.' I could see him computing in his head. Then he said, 'I want to come back here when I'm 24 and 48 and 96.' I know I can't be with him on those dates, so my dearest wish is that the wilderness will be here for him."

—Barbara Meyer speaking before a Congressional Committee considering designation of Ozark wilderness areas.

Above: Buffalo National River, Arkansas. Ducks find refuge on a mist-covered beaver pond in Boxley Valley on the upper Buffalo River.

Opposite: Goat Bluff, Buffalo National River. From high on a cliff, the canoeists below look like leaves floating on the emerald waters of the nation's first National River.

An Ozark Crusader Leads On

I had thought I would not have any trouble keeping up with an eighty-one-year-old man until I went hiking with Dr. Neil Compton. About twenty hikers from the Ozark Society follow Neil down an old wagon road, across a narrow ridgetop, and out onto Point Peter, a twenty-one-hundred-foot mountain overlooking the meandering Buffalo River. The view carries you all the way to Missouri. One thousand feet below, rows of sheer limestone bluffs rise out of the Buffalo, as the channel cuts its way toward the horizon. The scalloped ridge line of the Boston Mountains frames the wooded valley against the sky. On this winter day, ghostly splashes of white blooming serviceberry color the gray leafless slopes.

"Can you imagine this valley being a flat sea bottom?" Neil asks the group. "Millions of years ago, the Ozarkian Sea covered everything. Upheavals raised the land three times—not a whole lot compared to other mountain ranges, but enough for rivers to carve into the bedrock. This beautiful valley was formed by the hand of nature."

And preserved in large part by the hand of the man standing before us. Without the efforts of Dr. Compton and the Ozark Society, which he founded in 1962, this inspiring scene would once again be covered by a sea of water. During the decade-long bitter struggle against the dam builders, chronicled in Neil's book, *The Battle to Save the Buffalo*, the society confronted the most powerful political and economic forces in both the state and the nation.

"Everyone thought we were crazy," Neil says as we look across the valley. "The Corps of Engineers had been trying to dam the Buffalo since the early fifties; the state's most powerful Congressional representatives wanted the pork barrel project; and businessmen from Marshall, Arkansas, formed an association to aggressively lobby for the dam."

A classic David and Goliath struggle was shaping up when the Ozark Society stepped into the foray. In the heat of the struggle, Dr. Compton was physically threatened by an angry opponent as he spoke at a town meeting in Marshall, and he was shot at as he canoed the Buffalo with his daughter. On another occasion, extremists felled eighteen large trees across dangerous rapids to block an Ozark Society float trip. Neil also suffered from the stress and frustrations of dealing with Washington politics, as he and others in the Ozark Society tried to swing politicians to the conservationist side.

The Ozark Society grew from a few hundred members to three thousand, and its voice amplified from a whisper to a shout that could not be ignored. The society outlasted two presidents, three governors, and one House member, but the group tirelessly carried on the fight. Finally, on March 1, 1972, President Nixon signed the legislation sent up by Congress that freed the Buffalo River forever from the grips of the dam builders and created the nation's first national river. The city of Marshall now greets travelers with a canoe-shaped sign that proclaims the city as the "Gateway to the Buffalo."

So the view of the broad valley dissected by the free-flowing Buffalo is particularly satisfying for Neil Compton. "It's a special feeling to look at the river and

Opposite: Dr. Neil Compton, who was born in 1912 and served as the Washington County, Arkansas, health officer until he retired, organized the Ozark Society in the 1960s, and led the fight to save the Buffalo River from land developers and dam builders.

"To stand at the crest of Home Valley Bluff [on the Buffalo River] with the redbud and dog-wood in bloom, to behold the gorge of the Big Piney stretching away into the blue distance, is an experience second to none, the Grand Canyon notwithstanding."
—Dr. Neil Compton, founder of the Ozark Society.

Rush, Buffalo National River. So many prospectors hurried to the Buffalo River when zinc was discovered in 1880 that the boomtown was named Rush. The remains of the town, which lost its post office in the 1950s, is preserved by the National River.

remember all the effort that went into saving it. People thought we were trying the impossible. The Buffalo is a national treasure that we saved for future generations to enjoy. . . . I hope what we accomplished can serve as an example to other groups."

Neil did not set out to be a crusader; he just wanted to preserve the wonders of nature he had come to love in his native Ozarks. Born in 1912, he grew up on Coon Creek in Benton County, Arkansas. He studied zoology and geology as an undergraduate in Fayetteville, and earned his doctorate in medicine from the University of Arkansas in Little Rock.

"I didn't really start exploring the Ozarks until I returned from World War II," he recounts. "As the Washington County health officer, I learned from my patients about the natural wonders hidden away in the mountains. I took drive-abouts with my family and explored and photographed what we discovered."

Neil has never stopped exploring the land he loves. He still leads monthly outings for the Ozark Society to some of his favorite places in remote areas of the mountains. His personal experience and historical perspective make the trips far more than just a day hike or canoe ride. He reminisces about his youth in these mountains and entertains with folktales. His knowledge about nature and the

people of the Ozarks runs as freely as the river he helped save.

After visiting Point Peter, we head south on Highway 27. "People always talk about scenic Highway 7, but this road is prettier," he says as we wind through a narrow valley. "The Ozarks may not be as spectacular as Yosemite or Yellowstone, but . . . the forces that shaped the planet are evident in the hills and valleys. The Earth isn't frozen in death like the moon or Mars. The surface is changing all the time. . . . We can feel in our hearts that what we see here is the result of tremendous forces at work."

Neil champions the beauty of the Ozarks and crusades to save the sensitive mountain and river ecology at every chance. He finds willing ears among the seven chapters of the Ozark Society, which is established in four states. But one particular area of the wilderness continues to monopolize his efforts. The Buffalo River is just too close to his heart. "I'd like to see the entire watershed of the Buffalo . . . protected. Stopping the dams isn't enough if the river becomes too polluted for human contact."

His point is well made. According to the Arkansas Department of Pollution Control and Ecology, many streams in northwestern Arkansas periodically fail the water quality standards for "primary contact recreation," or swimming and walk-

Buffalo National River, Arkansas. Beaver Jim Villines, known for trapping beaver in the Buffalo River valley, was born in this log house in 1854. The structure has been stabilized and preserved by the National River.

The Buffalo River stands out as a superlative feature of the Ozark landscape, winding its way through scenes comparable with the Smokies, but on a smaller scale. It reminds me of a piece of the 'frontier.'"

—John D. Linahan, Superintendent, Buffalo National River

ing, mainly due to bacterial contamination from chicken farm and pasture run-off. The department's list regularly includes the most scenic streams in the Ozarks.

So, the work continues. Through the efforts of the Ozark Society and other conservation groups, four wilderness areas have been established on the upper and lower Buffalo to protect the creeks that flow into the river. Ten other wilderness areas preserve pristine portions of the Ozark and Mark Twain National Forests. Additionally, the Ozark National Scenic Riverways preserves 134 miles of the spring-fed Current and Jacks Fork Rivers in Missouri. Two other legislative designations, the federal "wild and scenic" and the state "extraordinary resource," protect a number of smaller streams in the Ozarks from damming, in-stream gravel mining, and other adverse development.

After eight decades of living in the Ozarks, Neil Compton is outspoken about saving his homeland. "Too many government programs are subsidizing the urbanization of the countryside," he says. "In the sixties and seventies, we had a chance to reverse some of the environmental damage. A lot of farmland was going back to nature. Then the government put power lines across the mountains and paved all the dirt roads so people could move back into areas that never should have been cleared."

Neil motions as we drive past several hundred acres of steep rolling hills recently bulldozed clean and the trees piled up to burn. "Anything overdone is an evil, and we are a nation of overdoers. We overdo paving roads, building dams, and raising chicken and cattle in an area nature meant to be a forest. The government subsidizes farmers with tax write-offs to turn the forest into a monoculture of fescue grass. Bulldozers cause more destruction than clear-cutting ever did in the national forests. What we are seeing is the Ozarkian desert being formed by human folly."

I ask Dr. Compton what he would like to see happen by the year 2000. "I'd like to see the return of the forest cover to the Ozark Mountains. The Ozarks once were the best source of hardwoods in the world, especially the oaks, hickories, and walnuts in the White River Valley. But the Forest Service isn't replanting hardwoods. The only ones planting walnuts are the squirrels."

Neil retired as a physician in 1978, but his years of service have never slowed. His long list of awards include an honorary doctorate in law from his Fayetteville alma mater, the University of Arkansas, and numerous community service and conservation awards. President Bush presented him with the Teddy Roosevelt Conservation Award in 1990. Last fall, the Arkansas Library Association presented him with the Arkansiana Award for his two books on the Ozarks.

The next day, Neil leads the group on a four-mile hike down an unmarked, unnamed trail to a spectacular rock formation known to locals as Buzzard's Roost. At age eighty-one, he shows no signs of slowing down. As members of the Ozark Society attest, keeping pace with the good doctor, on the trail or in battling for the environment, is not an easy task.

Springwater and Changing Times

"'Goin' to the mill'... was also an opportunity to visit with seldom-seen neighbors and catch up on the neighborhood news. Since long lines at the mill were common, whole families went along and sometimes even camped out while awaiting their turn. While they took advantage of the enforced rest, they could enjoy the fellowship of their neighbors."
—Phyllis Rossiter, 1992, *A Living History of the Ozarks.*

"The world is but one country and mankind its citizens."
—Bahá'u'lláh, founder of the Bahá'i Faith

Above: Oregon County, Missouri. Greer Spring, the third largest in the Ozarks, pumps out 217 million gallons a day. One channel gushes from beneath a rocky bluff; the other, shown here, boils up in the streambed.

Opposite: Ozark County, Missouri. When travel was limited to wagons, local grist mills thrived in the spring-rich Ozarks. The few still standing, like the Hodgson Mill near Sycamore, recall a time when people lived out their lives within a fifty-mile radius of their birthplace.

Above: Shannon County, Missouri. Forty-seven million gallons of aquamarine water a day pour from Blue Spring into the Current River.

Opposite: Ozark National Forest, Stone County, Arkansas. The underground stream in Blanchard Springs Caverns emerges from a limestone bluff to form Mirror Lake. The caverns, maintained by the National Forest Service, are among the most spectacular in the nation.

Springs, Gristmills, and the Twenty-First Century

The Ozark Mountains cannot be separated from the springs that nourish its streams, rivers, and lakes, and the caves that lace its subterranean depths. The porous, limestone mountains receive between forty and fifty inches of rain per year. After carving the valleys and nourishing the numerous springs, the rainwater dissolves the limestone bedrock and forms vast karst, or cave, systems. Missouri boasts some 5,000 known caverns, 20 with guided tours, and Arkansas sits on top of another 1,000 to 1,500. Onondaga Cave at Onondaga State Park near Leasburg, Missouri, and Blanchard Springs Caverns near Mountain View, Arkansas, in the Ozark National Forest, are two spectacular examples of nature's underground handiwork. In addition, caves have played a prominent role in the history and heritage of the Ozarks. Tom Sawyer's fictitious exploits in what is now Mark Twain Cave, near Hannibal, Missouri; the Jessie James hideout in Meramec Caverns, near Stanton, Missouri; and the Depression-era moonshine stills that were hidden in the sinkholes and rock shelters, are only a few examples of the connection between the caverns and the colorful past of the Ozarks.

The honeycombed, limestone foundation of the Ozark Mountains soaks up the abundant rainfall like a sponge and creates one large superaquifer. Within a fifty-mile radius of Eminence, Missouri, springs with enormous volume feed the Spring, Current, Jacks Fork, and Eleven Point Rivers. The Current and Jacks

"I remember the wet, cool springs in the Ozarks. Wandering up the trail to Hidden Valley, walking through blooming dogwoods and redbuds, rounding a bend in the trail to a sparkling waterfall."

—Richard Mason, former president of the Arkansas Wildlife Federation.

Fork form the 134-mile-long Ozarks National Scenic Riverways, the first streams so designated in the nation.

Big Spring, near Van Buren, Missouri, is the largest single outlet spring in the United States. It averages 275 million gallons per day, but at times pours as much as 840 million gallons of water per day into the Current River. But the source of the river is a more modest 43-million-gallon-per-day spring ninety miles upstream at Montauk State Park. Every morning, scores of fishermen line the three miles of riverbanks in the park. Just a few casts into the stream will usually hook one of the hundreds of rainbow trout released by the adjacent hatchery. The park also preserves an 1896 gristmill. Overall, fifty large springs feed the Current and Jacks Fork river system.

Three major springs surround the hamlet of Eminence near the convergence of the two rivers. At Round Spring, you can take a guided tour through Round Spring Cave that winds along a one-mile trail decorated with beautiful formations. Blue Spring produces the deepest blue water of any spring in the Ozarks. Forty-seven million gallons of the aquamarine water flow into the Current River every day. A three-story roller mill, constructed in 1894, still stands at Alley Spring. It used a turbine instead of the traditional waterwheel to supply power for grinding grain. You can camp and picnic beside this 81 million-gallon-per-day spring that flows into the Jacks Fork River. The Ozark National Scenic Riverways maintains camping and recreational facilities at eight springs and access points along the two rivers.

With an abundance of spring-fed rivers and steep topography, the Ozarks provided millers with an ample supply of waterfalls and constant steams to power their grinding stones. Once while hiking miles from the closest dirt road in Richland Wilderness, near the Buffalo River, I discovered two lichen-covered millstones in a creek bottom. The fact that a farming community had thrived so far into what is now dense wilderness attests both to the widespread penetration of the early settlers, and to how well the forest has healed from the logging and clear-cutting activities of the past century. The stones reportedly came from France in the 1890s, but were never put to use. Of the dreams and aspirations, hopes and labor of the settlers, only two lichen-covered millstones remain.

A short trail off Highway 19 south of Eminence leads along a virgin pine-oak ridge to the headwaters of Greer Springs. Its output of 217 million gallons per day makes it the second largest in Missouri. You can hear the roar of the spring long before reaching the rocky bluff overlooking the gushing water. Water flows from a cave at the foot of the bluff with such intensity that it creates surflike waves and rapids. Just downstream another outlet bubbles up midstream like a boiling caldron. The flow has carved a one-mile gorge seventy feet deep, and supplies 60 percent of the Eleven Point River flowing at that location. An abandoned 1899 gristmill stands downstream, in view of the road but inaccessible to the public.

Farther north along Missouri Highway 19, a small sign reads, "Falling Water Spring." Instead of plunging over a waterfall, this spring emerges from a rock face as though Moses had struck it with his staff. The spring pours 500,000 gallons per day from the fissure halfway up the sheer bluff.

Mark Twain National Forest, Oregon County, Missouri. The gristmill at Falling Water Spring once milled as many as ten wagonloads of corn a day. The spring still pours out 500,000 gallons of water per day beside the silent mill.

The plentiful water of the Ozarks welcomed the first settlers like the promises of a whispering lover. Valleys with rich soil and dependable springs and streams soon became bustling centers of commerce. For more than a century, the Falling Water Spring gristmill serviced area farmers. As many as ten wagonloads at a time parked along the road awaiting their turn. The metal wheel of the gristmill dates back to the 1920s and once ground corn and feed, sawed shingles and firewood, and generated electricity for the site. Thomas and Jane Brown homesteaded the spring site in 1851 and lived in a one-room log cabin. Remnants of their home, barn, and blacksmith shed still remain. In the adjacent cemetery, the gravestones record the mortal comings and goings of nineteenth-century residents of the region.

Standing in the shade of the old cabin with the spring pouring steadily from the rocky bluff and the weathered mill reflecting in the pond, you can catch a glimpse of what life was like when the gristmill was in operation. You can almost hear the sounds of children playing and families visiting echo across the still waters, while the waterwheel creaks and grinds the year's harvest into meal. Gathering by the spring provided the perfect opportunity for the hard-working farmers to socialize and catch up on the community news after a summer of intensive labor.

In the decentralized agricultural society prior to World War II, unpaved, rutted wagon roads were the only routes in and out of the remote hollows of the Ozarks. As most people seldom ventured more than fifty miles from their place of birth, every fertile valley needed a gristmill. Today, many of the Ozark gristmills still stand beside flowing streams and waterfalls, their wheels as silent as the placid ponds that mirror their reflection.

The abandoned mills that dot the Ozark streams represent a radical change in lifestyle that transformed rural America by the end of World War II. At the beginning of this century, families living on farms and in self-sufficient communities populated the countryside. Mills ground locally grown grain, and markets sold locally grown vegetables. Blacksmith shops produced parts to repair wagons and machinery, and local artisans crafted furniture and houseware items. With long-distance transportation limited to trains and tortuous roads, communities made do with goods produced in nearby settlements.

When in 1932 Ozark historian and folklorist Wayman Hogue wrote *Back Yonder, An Ozark Chronicle*, he could say, "The self-sufficiency and rugged independence of the American pioneer days exists today in the Ozarks, almost untouched by Machine Age economics and material improvements. . . . There, in an empire of their own, far removed from the conventionalities, the disadvantages, and the problems of 'civilization,' they are living the peaceful, free and easy life that they lived 50 years ago, and that they will continue for a 100 years to come."

Time may seem to stand still as we float down one of the pristine Ozark streams surrounded by the unchanging beauty of nature, but the abandoned gristmills remind us that life has changed rapidly and dramatically. Today, our fresh vegetables come, not from our own gardens, but from California or Mexico or continents farther south, and most of our clothes and manufactured items originate in Asia. Computers, satellite dishes, fiber-optic communication, and scores of other products of the Machine Age routinely shape everyday life in even the remotest valleys. The pioneer spirit and rugged independence still exist, and the streams still run clear, though not as pure. But as the twenty-first century dawns, the "Ozark empire" Hogue described has all but vanished. We all, including the people of the highest hills and deepest hollows of the Ozarks, have become world citizens, whether we are ready to embrace that perspective or not.

"The Missouri Ozarks was a great place to grow up. As a kid, I was never far from the beautiful timbered, rolling hills and clean, clear running streams. I have especially fond memories of time spent with my father, seining minnows, collecting crayfish, or float fishing the James and White rivers. As I grew older, I enjoyed, as I still do, fishing our Ozark lakes for smallmouth and largemouth bass."
**—John L. Morris,
Bass Pro Shops**

Index

Suggested Readings

Compton, Neil. *The High Ozarks.* Little Rock, AR: Ozark Society Foundation, 1982.

———. *Battle for the Buffalo River: A Twentieth Century Crisis in the Ozarks.* Fayetteville: University of Arkansas Press, 1992.

Deane, Ernie. *Ozarks Country.* Branson, MO: The Ozark Mountaineer, 1975. Sales of this book benefit the Ernie Deane Memorial Journalism Fund at the University of Arkansas. You can order a copy for $6.95 plus postage from Frances Deane Alexander, 910 Arlington Terrace, Fayetteville, AR 72701.

Ernst, Tim. *Arkansas Portfolio.* Fayetteville, AR: Tim Ernst Photography, 1995.

———. *Hiking Buffalo River Trails.* Fayetteville, AR: Tim Ernst Photography, 1991.

Gass, Ramon. *Missouri Hiking Trails.* Jefferson City: Missouri Department of Conservation, 1990.

Henry, Steve. *The Mountain Biker's Guide to the Ozarks.* Birmingham, AL: Menasha Ridge Press, 1993.

Hogue, Wayman. *Back Yonder: An Ozark Chronicle.* New York: Minton, Balch & Co., 1932.

Jameson, W.C. *Buried Treasures of the Ozarks.* Little Rock, AR: August House, 1990.

McDonough, Nancy. *Garden Sass: A Catalog of Arkansas Folkways.* New York: Coward, McCann, & Geoghegann, 1975.

Rafferty, Milton. *The Ozarks: Land and Life.* Norman: University of Oklahoma Press, 1980.

Rossiter, Phyllis. *A Living History of the Ozarks.* Gretna, LA: Pelican, 1992.

Smith, Kenneth. *Buffalo River Country.* Little Rock, AR: Ozark Society Foundation, 1967.

Where to go for More Information

Oregon County, Missouri. Highway 19 south of Winona rolls with the undulating terrain of the Springfield Plateau of the Ozark Mountains.

ARKANSAS DEPARTMENT OF PARKS AND TOURISM. One Capitol Mall, Little Rock, AR 72201. Phone 501-682-7777 or toll-free at 800-NATU-RAL. Information available: state parks, travel destination booklets, vacation kit.

BUFFALO NATIONAL RIVER. P.O. Box 1173, Harrison, AR 72602-1173. Phone 501-741-5443. Information available: floating, camping, and hiking on and along the river.

BRANSON HOTLINE: Phone 800-523-7589. Information available: entertainment options and ticket reservations.

MARK TWAIN NATIONAL FOREST. 401 Fairgrounds Road, Rolla, MO 65401. Phone 314-364-4621. Information available: camping and hiking in the forests.

MISSOURI DEPARTMENT OF NATURAL RESOURCES. Division of State Parks, P.O. Box 176, Jefferson City, MO 65102. Phone 314-751-3443 or toll-free at 800-334-6946. Information available: state parks booklet.

MISSOURI DIVISION OF TOURISM. P.O. Box 1055, Jefferson City, MO 65102. Phone 314-751-4133 or toll-free at 800-877-1234. Information available: travel destination booklets.

OZARK NATIONAL FOREST. P.O. Box 1008, Russellville, AR 72811. Phone 501-968-2354. Information available: camping and hiking in the forests.

OZARKS NATIONAL SCENIC RIVERWAYS. P.O. Box 490, Van Buren, MO 63965. Phone 314-323-4236. Information available: floating, camping, and hiking on and along the rivers.

About the Author

George Oxford Miller is a Little Rock–based nature writer and photographer. He has authored six books in addition to *The Ozarks*, including *The Texas Hill Country* and *Landscaping with Native Plants of Texas and the Southwest* for Voyageur Press. His articles on environmental topics have appeared in numerous magazines and newspapers, and his column "Austin Au Natural" won the National Audubon Society's Annual Conservation Award. He has led nature and photography tours throughout North and Central America, and he has taught photography at the University of Texas and the University of Arkansas at Little Rock. He currently is editor of the Arkansas Arts Chronicle magazine.

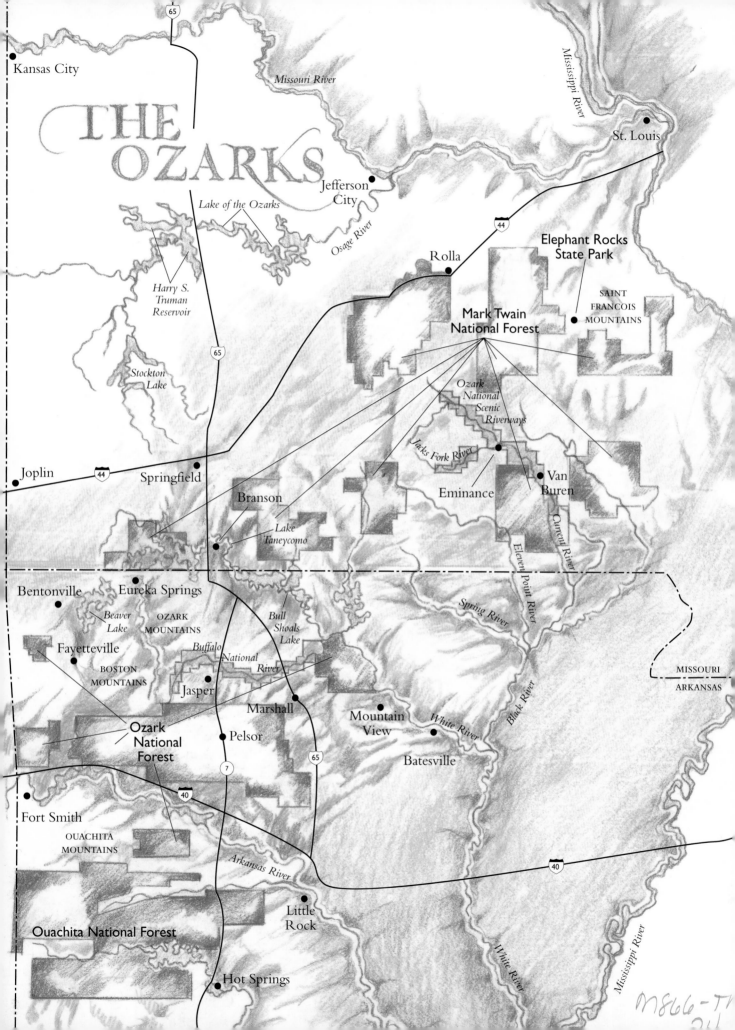

THE OZARKS

Kansas City

Missouri River

Mississippi River

St. Louis

Jefferson City

Lake of the Ozarks

Rolla

Elephant Rocks State Park

Osage River

SAINT FRANCOIS MOUNTAINS

Harry S. Truman Reservoir

Mark Twain National Forest

Ozark National Scenic Riverways

Stockton Lake

Jacks Fork River

Joplin

Springfield

Eminance

Van Buren

Branson

Lake Taneycomo

Curent River

Eleven Point River

Bentonville

Eureka Springs

Beaver Lake

OZARK MOUNTAINS

Bull Shoals Lake

Spring River

Black River

MISSOURI

ARKANSAS

Fayetteville

Buffalo

National River

BOSTON MOUNTAINS

Jasper

Marshall

Mountain View

White River

Ozark National Forest

Pelsor

Batesville

Fort Smith

OUACHITA MOUNTAINS

Arkansas River

Little Rock

Ouachita National Forest

Hot Springs

White River

Mississippi River

M866-T/